Dark

Psychology

Influence People And Become A
Leader

Johnson L Brock

Published By **John Kembrey**

Johnson L Brock

Dark Psychology: Influence People And Become A Leader

ISBN   978-1-998769-54-4

No part of this guidebook shall be reproduced in any form without permission in writing from the publisher except in the case of brief quotations embodied in critical articles or reviews.

Legal & Disclaimer

The information contained in this ebook is not designed to replace or take the place of any form of medicine or professional medical advice. The information in this ebook has been provided for educational & entertainment purposes only.

The information contained in this book has been compiled from sources deemed reliable, and it is accurate to the best of the Author's knowledge; however, the Author cannot guarantee its accuracy and validity and cannot be held liable for any errors or omissions. Changes are periodically made to this book. You must consult your doctor or get professional medical advice before using any of the suggested remedies, techniques, or information in this book.

Table Of Contents

Introduction

Dark psychology is an important sub-specialty of psychology that is often misunderstood. It studies the hidden forces that shape who we are and how these forces can be used to control, coerce, and punish. It can be applied to seemingly disparate areas, such as philosophy and sociology, anthropology, or criminal psychology. Dark psychology also focuses on psychology and criminal behaviour as seen from the perspective of an aggressor. It appeals to those who are intrigued by the power and influence of social media, human vulnerability, as well as covert tactics that are often called black magic.

Dark psychology is a form of applied philosophy, though its origins are not clear. These concepts were quickly studied by sociologists to discover how these subtle influences could affect entire societies. It was inevitable that these ideas would eventually become a part of popular culture, where they would be adopted and used by occultists for their personal benefit or against enemies.

Like psychology, there is no consensus as to what dark psychology is or how it should look. Most sources agree it is mainly composed of two main groups. These are hidden forces (non-verbal communication), second orders conditioning (in the sense that mental states can alter someone else's), rhetorical language and sociopathic cognitions. Manipulation techniques or tactics that exploit human vulnerabilities to gain self-gain at others' expense.

Dark psychology techniques are most frequently mentioned.

Emotional Manipulation

This is called second-order conditioning. Emotions are tied to people or situations so that it is difficult for an individual to separate. Emotional manipulation can often be done by implicit associations. This means that one stimulus may elicit an emotion, but these emotions can then be associated with another stimulus. You might find it difficult to laugh at other people's jokes if you first associate laughing with your enjoyment. This can also happen by controlling the primary stimuli.

A man could be made to hate his job by peer pressure. This would make it hard for the man to be happy while working. Many people have experienced miserable jobs and know that the best thing to do is get fired.

Emotional manipulation works due to the fact that emotions can be powerful triggers of behavior. If we are confronted by emotions, we often do more than we intended. According to Richard Boyatzis, Daniel Goleman, and Richard Boyatzis in Fire in the Brain: the Role of Emotions in Decstructive and Creative Behaviors, "Reactivity is the strongest aspect and the most powerful motivator of human behavior." Though most people do not know that others manipulate

3

them, powerful manipulators like psychopaths might incite behaviors without any deliberate intention.

Systolic Rage

This is a second-order form of conditioning in which an individual's primary emotions become so intense they cause a feeling that they are causing rage. All of us have experienced this, whether we are angry about injustices or feel strongly negative responses to certain situations. It can feel dangerous to explode or seriously harm someone when anger is intense.

Others can also use the arousal or systolic passion to cause emotional reactions in their friends and family. These emotional responses can cause people to do something they might not have done otherwise (e.g. revenge). This theme is common in many movies and books. However it is not easy to make happen without second order conditioning.

Karma

This is the notion that there is a balance between karma (or "the law governing cause and effect"), which may seem abstract at first. However, dark practitioners have used it for centuries as a way of getting certain responses from their victim(e.g. to control their willingness or inability to perform an action). You are often told that if you do wrong to someone, it will always return at you later. People believe this because it is something they have been taught from a young age and read many times about it in various sources.

It can be seen that this subtle encouragement of bad behaviour is a way of devaluing victim or victim's response under poor treatment. Sometimes, it may be a way to convince others that the victim is not worthy of the treatment they receive.

Sociopaths

Individuals who do not live up to their moral standards or care little about the well-being and welfare of others. These people may use other people to gain personal advantage and manipulate others for their own ends. They will also not show any remorse or guilt, even when they are wrong. This is a controversial opinion as sociologists argue that there are many types who could be called sociopaths.

Most dark psychology practitioners don't believe all sociopaths have to be evil. However, dark psychology practitioners do recognize that some people may have psychopathic tendencies if they are able to use complex tactics to accomplish their goals. This ability is often found in people who take a childlike approach and act the part even when it is against their ideals.

Today, manipulation tactics are used all the time in daily life. Some people use them to get what they want, others to defend themselves from harm. Sometimes we don't even realize that others are using them on our behalf. However, they can be very dangerous and have a profound affect on our lives. You need to watch what happens and make sure that it is consistent with your ideas and our conduct code. You should also evaluate whether the motivation behind your actions is motivated by love and compassion, or if it's more selfishly motivated to reach an agenda.

Manipulation strategies are very effective because they make the most of human nature. These manipulation tactics stem from our basic instincts as well as our desire for acceptance and approval from others. In some cases they may even be based upon society's "norm" or "right." A person might not realize they are manipulating someone until later.

There are many benefits to refusing to accept manipulation tactics or misdirections as a normal way of life. These tactics will not be noticed as we are more skilled at recognizing them in other people than ourselves. We can also prevent being controlled or controlled by others who use them.

Meditation can also be a great way to improve your mental discipline and self-awareness. It is hard to understand the motivations behind one's actions without these skills. These are skills that we now need more than ever in this world, so it's worth learning if your goal is to live a happy life.

Chapter 1: Understanding Manipulation

Manipulation, a type social influence, aims to alter the behavior of others.

These techniques could be considered devious and exploitative because they serve the manipulator's interests, often at great cost to another.

Social influence or impact could be considered underhanded manipulation, depending on context and motivations. But the concept of exercise does not necessarily mean that social influence is negative. Use basic tools to your benefit. Ask your questions and make the most of your time.

Asking questions will help you redirect your attention back to your manipulator. They don't expect to be asked questions by you, especially if their manipulators have already been manipulating. This can be a way for them to get out of control and force them to realize they are playing a dangerous game.

You'll have to get them to regroup or flip the tables, and then use another tactic.

If someone is trying to manipulate or force you to do something, it's easy to say something like "I'll have a think about it." Your manipulator will expect you to think, but not do, on a normal basis. When you don't agree to their demands, it can be a way to stir them up and confuse them.

A second way to handle manipulation is to avoid people or places that make it uncomfortable. Stay away from manipulators if you are certain. At least until you are able either to control their behavior or ignore it. Stay away from places you are uncomfortable in, where people are trying to make you do things that you don't want. If you trust your instincts, it will make your life easier.

One of the biggest problems for the target is to take blame or feel like something is wrong. This is exactly the goal of a manipulator. It is possible to be positive and not believe everything the manipulator wants you to believe. It doesn't matter what they tell, but you need to step back and be confident in your own abilities. Positive energy can overcome their negative energy. Let their words and actions wash over your without allowing them in.

Important things to remember when it comes to your manipulator

They are most often just bullies.

A manipulator will typically back down if your foot is down. They love people who are compliant and easy to control. They are most likely to give up when it becomes difficult.

The manipulator is often also a victim. This is how they get along. Although it doesn't make things right, it can help you to see the bigger picture. Someone who feels powerless or unable to control their own life wants to be in control. They seek out someone they think is weaker than their own and they target them. They feel stronger and less vulnerable.

Or, they can be manipulators without any explanation. It is impossible to change them but it is possible to overpower them and allow them to control your life.

Once you have taken control, you will need to set boundaries. Boundaries are crucial, especially for those who have to deal with you regularly. You cannot take them out completely of your life. If they are a threat to your life, it is important to establish boundaries and set the consequences for them not following those boundaries. This shows them you are serious, and may cause them to consider you weak. Be consistent. As a child, if your fingers slip even once, your manipulator will give you a pass and keep pushing the limits.

What Is Manipulation, You Ask?

Manipulation involves manipulating other people's behavior, thoughts, and actions to make them do what you want. While you may think it's selfish, there is an element of drive in every wrongdoing. Manipulation could therefore be used in a positive manner. You can see this in the way a good DJ attempts to mix different musical styles together in order to demonstrate his ability to blend them into a harmonious sound for the audience. It is almost unfair to each song's original creator. An individual who is skilled in manipulating words, emotions, feelings, and thoughts would be able achieve their main wish.

A plan and indirect scheme to manipulate people could be used. Periodic manipulation can be described as telling a friend that someone is looking great when they are feeling mentally or physically depressed. This is technically complex as it can impact your friend's perception of you. This will ultimately affect how they relate with you. Manipulation can also be linked to emotional abuse, particularly when it occurs in very close relationships. Depending upon your perspective, manipulation may be considered to be negative if it causes harm to the individual being manipulated. On the other hand, manipulative people can argue that manipulative individuals can control their environment and subordinate others. Also manipulators can find it hard to relate to their true selves. This could lead to negative consequences for an individual.

The three major types of manipulation that you need to be able to comprehend are: There is the manipulation of options. In this case, the environment's options can be altered with rewards or threats. The second is information manipulation. In this case, the individual's perceptions of the environment are altered in order to alter their understanding. Psychological manipulation also refers to the influence of someone that results in a change or improvement in their mental cognition.

In manipulative encounters there are four main components: the hearer and listener; the motive and covertness of the speaker; and the interest of their speaker. These are called prerequisites to manipulation. Any type of manipulation is intended to have an effect on a target or listener. The target may act in an opposite way to what he used before being manipulated. A manipulative situation means that the manipulator sees more clearly than the target.

This is what defines manipulation. Intent determines the extent to which the target has been manipulated. It is important to know the intention of the speaker, as it could be harmful for the listener. Communication usually involves the speaker, the hearer and the speaker's motives.

The widespread view of manipulation must remain secretive in order for it to hold. To a large degree, I believe that manipulation can be traced back to the motive of the speaker. It is designed to meet the speaker's interest and desires. I can also confirm that manipulative mechanisms are related to manipulator motives.

It is vital to recognize that manipulations can be performed unconsciously or without being aware. Some people manipulate intentionally.

Intentional manipulators, however, can be very tricky. They will brag about their skills because they are well aware. The manipulator can be cunning, smart and cunny simultaneously through the game of manipulation. They tend to be self-centered and cannot be trusted with caring for others.

Diverse Forms Of Manipulation

Resistance to demands from others can come in the form of making excuses or blaming others.

Indirect threats or implied threats Example: A mother might give a scathing look to her child for leaving their dirty uniform on a floor.

Character or behavior that is deceitful includes fraud, fabrication, corruption, and even theft.

Selfishness in disseminating useful information. One example is if you know someone who needs a job and you receive information about companies with vacancies.

She is making someone else leave a company/association of loved ones. This could be a single mother who is angry at her father or isolates her child from his family.

To attempt to change someone's belief. This can lead often to misdirection, denial, or low self-esteem.

Forcefully criticizing, insulting and denouncing another person. Bullying is one example.

The sexual intercourse method is used to achieve a goal. This is a common practice among employees and employers.

But, manipulation can lead to poor mental health. Chronic manipulation could lead to anxiety, depression, wrong coping techniques, lying, and difficulty trusting others. This could cause a victim to lose their values and question their reality. Gaslight, a classic movie depicting the manipulation of a husband to a wife in subtly subtle ways, illustrates this situation. He manipulates her so that she doesn't rely on her perceptions. The man secretly turned off the gaslights and made his wife believe she was seeing things dimly.

Manipulators also have a way of making their victim feel good, even though they aren't always truthful. These manipulators use their skill to make a deep and intimate connection with people. To manipulate a victim, they will use their power in an unfair manner. They will go to great lengths to ensure they get what their desires.

There are subtle signals that can be detected from you and others. Some examples include being naive and acting nice and charming all the while. At some point in our lives we are all tempted to lie. To manipulate people, you may tell a lie in order to make them happy or get out of a difficult situation. Some people see it as a way of life.

You probably know that manipulators are all around you. You should ask yourself, what personalities do they have? A manipulator could be your neighbor who spreads gossip about you. They could also be members of your family who make others insecure or create chaos. So anyone can manipulate you. They are usually criminals that use tricks to distract from your possessions.

The Behavior Traits Of Favorite Victims

Sensitive People

But power is only one component in manipulation. While power can be used to manipulate others, it is only a part of manipulating people. The manipulator is the one with more power than others and who is not able to get their desired results through mutual agreements or other means. He/she resorts to manipulative tactics that often result in manipulation.

You can neutralize their emotional manipulation by not caring what the other person feels or says. This allows you to counter the power they hold over you. It is not possible to compel someone to do something using external force. And if the aggressor believes that you may suffer physical harm as a result of refusing to grant a request, you have a problem more than just emotional manipulation. Emotional manipulation, however, has the power within to compel. You have two options. The first one can either be detrimental to your self-esteem or help you see that you have full control over what happens in your own mind. Don't allow anyone to dictate what happens inside.

You have ultimate control over your destiny. It is up to you to make that a habit.

Empathic People

An empathic person absorbs more emotion then the average person. If they are able to sense emotions in a way that is more than the average person, their slighted suspicion that you would like them to do something will be magnified and they will go about doing it to feel better. However, the empath is not in control of the empath.

It is becoming more common that women are empathic and more accepting of others. That is not a bad thing. But if you remind someone that they are who they really are, they can be manipulated more easily.

All it takes to make you feel beautiful, sexy, or stunning is to weaken your intellect. This can happen at all times, though it may not be the case every time. Women can be manipulated by men who give them obsequious or compliments in order to take advantage of their situation. They don't break because they get compliments and gifts. It's the reminder of who they are as women that breaks them.

You need to improve your mindset before the event. It's a similar process to building the walls of medieval cities. You don't build walls right when marauding armies arrive.

Alter the stereotypes that you have about your gender and yourself. When you do that, it is much more difficult for anyone to try to convince you to change. When you think about the art of enslaving people in modern times, it is possible for a handful of slave owners to control hundreds of slaves. Why? What if the slaves can overpower them by numbers? They can't because their mind has been manipulated.

You can protect your mind and your thought and you'll be able to stop a large portion of the manipulating attackers.

Fear of Loneliness

If a victim is feeling lonely, in desperate need for comfort and support, they are more likely to receive love bombings at a higher level than other victims. If the victim is more grounded, they may need to be love-bombed in a more subtle and less intense way.

Working with love bombing means that the manipulator will feel a strong sense of affection, trust and compliance. The way the manipulator views the situation will affect the extent of love bombing and the outcome.

Fear of Disapointing Others

Imagine your insecurity leading you to believe negative thoughts that lead to undesirable behaviors. Your partner might feel some of the negative effects of insecurity. It may take time but it will happen.

Signs Of Instability

Here are 6 signs that instabilities might be impacting your connection according to professionals.

These anxieties, which are vanity-based, can cause instability. We worry about how others view us, and we don't feel confident in our own abilities and self-worth. These are signs you should be aware of to recognize your own insecurities and to stop listening to the ego.

1. Flaunting

Bluffing about what you have done and how much you have accomplished is one of the main indicators of instability. Troubled people often try to make others happy. They are then unable to get recognition from the outside. If you are able to feel safe and secure within yourself, you will not be compelled to make others happy. You also don't require validation from others.

2. Regulating

Monitoring individuals can sometimes appear stable. But anxiety and also insecurity are the main causes of controlling behavior. It is one of the most frequent indicators of instability. If we fear we will not be able deal with the unexpected, we try to control the environment around us. We also attempt to maintain safe and secure boundaries to keep us risk-free. It can also lead to us trying to control other people. We only feel safe when they behave in predictable ways. Understanding that life can be handled, no matter what happens, means we no longer feel the need for control. Then, we are able to let go of control and allow life to unfold as it does.

3. Anxiety and stress

Anxiety can be caused by the fear of not being good enough. Anxiety is often caused by fear of the opinions of others or the fear that we might be judged. Individuals who are confident in their ability to protect themselves from danger don't worry about these things as often. This is because they don't insist on being right every time. While they may have high expectations for themselves, they don't let that stop them from making mistakes. They are aware that they are only human and may make mistakes.

4. Individuals that are kind

Uncertainty is manifested by the constant need to please others. This is a hinderance to living your own life. Sometimes it can seem that your life doesn't belong to you if you constantly try to make people happy. High self-esteem individuals show compassion and empathy for others. They don't feel responsible or responsible for someone else's happiness. It is true. You are not responsible if another person is satisfied.

If you are someone who is always looking out for others, then you need to make time for yourself. You must have the freedom to do what makes your heart happy. However, people-pleasing may lead to bitterness or even martyrdom. This is not a healthy or balanced way to live. People-pleasing not only is harmful for you but it can also be detrimental for others.

Chapter 2: Dark Persuasion

Persuasion exists all around us. People use it every day. Everyday they see ads on TV that attempt to convince them. They will likely meet salespeople on the streets and in stores trying to sell them something. Persuasion is essential for maintaining control and gaining support in politics as well as churches. It is everywhere you turn. It is almost everywhere you look. Persuasion may not seem as intrusive as manipulation but it is still important.

You might think this: Is being able convince someone is a bad trait if you are a salesperson? Do persuasiveness and lobbying are bad things? You can be persuasive as long you do it legally and ethically. You might find it beneficial to learn the art and science behind persuasion. With more persuasiveness, you will be able sell more, get more people to sign your petition, and vote for you.

Principles of Persuasion

Before we get into the details of dark persuasion and how it works, let's first look at how persuasion works. Persuasion involves six key principles. These principles work together, making your chances of convincing someone else much greater than if you don't implement them. These six principles are:

Consistency & commitment

People love consistency. It provides predictability and allows everyone to do things in a predictable way. People like those who are consistent because they are reliable and trustworthy. Trustworthiness, which is a highly valuable skill, is extremely important. People also prefer consistency to unpredictability. Consistency is what people seek to be viewed as. This can be very helpful if you are able to see the possibilities for persuading others.

Consistency is not enough to convince someone. You need to appeal to their commitment first. As important as consistency, commitments are essential to people. People who break commitments are frequently viewed as unstable or unreliable. They are just as valuable as people who are reliable. You can influence people by using commitment. The best way to do this is to convince them to commit. It doesn't make a difference what they commit too--anything is fine. One example is asking your coworker in the office to shred some documents for you. He may say he's going to shred documents at the back. If he consents, you might ask him to make some copies for you. He may accept, as it takes him only a few more seconds to complete the task and he will be back there already. If he is in the backroom, you may ask him to brew fresh espresso. You might also agree with him using the same logic: he is already back in the back room and has already said he will do something else. You have the coworker now completing at most 15 minutes of your work because he had made one commitment, and then wanted to continue saying yes.

Use dark persuasion to win the first commitment. Then, ask the person to continue asking until you reach the desired result. Your coworker would have laughed at your request to make coffee, to shred documents and to copy several documents. Instead, you persuaded him to do so by appealing for consistency and commitment.

Scarcity

People are extremely fickle. They tend to be more interested when they don't have it or believe they won't get it. When a cafe or restaurant takes something that isn't popular off the menu, for example. In order to make people more interested in something, it is possible to artificially create a shortage. People are more likely to miss something when it is no longer possible, even though they were not interested in it previously.

Many restaurants profit from this trend by creating rotating menus. They may offer limited-time items, but advertise they will return within a week. This accomplishes two things: it gets people into the restaurant/store, and even though they run out of the limited-time item quickly, they don't lose any money. The restaurant will earn even more by having them buy another product since they already spent their time getting there.

When persuading others, you can use scarcity to your advantage by appealing for limitations. Make it clear that the deal you're trying to convince others is for a limited period of time. You should also make it a point not to mention what might happen if they do not accept the deal. People will be more willing to sign up if you highlight what is at risk. They do not want loss and are more likely be pressured to sign a poor deal to avoid losing.

Reciprocity

Reciprocity simply means that if you do something good for me, I will also do my best to help you. It's the act of giving back favors. It is when someone holds the door to the store for you so you can go out. If they hold the door, it is likely that you will open the second door to let them in. This concept is that all favors should be returned in the interest of benefiting everyone. Remember the discussion about empathy? You know that selfless acts can lead to more selfless actions, which in turn makes people more likely survive.

Persuasion is a way to tap into this thought process. People will feel obligated if you do something to help them. This can be even though it is an inconvenience to them and may even cause them to stop trying to do what you want. If you create a sense of obligation, you can get what your heart desires, even though they might not agree with you in normal circumstances.

Dark persuasion allows you to make use of this. Persuasion is the act of persuading someone to do X because they will be benefited. You are trying to get something out the exchange by using dark persuasion.

While you want what you want, ethically, you do not want others to benefit.

To make the most of this opportunity, first ask your coworker to do something in exchange. Then, ask what you would like to receive. To give an example, if your coworker is willing to work on Saturday, offer to do the following: Take out the trash, clean the bathrooms, and maybe help your coworker with the cleaning. She will gladly allow you to do so. You ask her about Saturday work, knowing that she loves to be free for fun with friends. Simply because you did the actual dirty work earlier in the day, she will be more likely to say yes.

Likability

People will often go out of their way to help friends and family members they feel connected to, rather than helping strangers. The closer you feel to someone, the more willing you will be to help them. It means you are much more likely than others to persuade you if your friends and family are like you. It's easy to be liked. There are three main factors that will determine whether someone is likable or not. You are much more likely to like someone if they do these three key things.

You can convince others to like what you know by simply understanding these three aspects. This skill can be useful beyond persuading others. You can use it to convince them to invite you into their lives. If someone trusts you and you demonstrate that your goal is common, they are much more likely be to allow you into their inner circle.

Social proof

Social proof is, at its core, the concept and practice of peer pressure. It's the notion that people will give in to peer pressure when they are not sure how to act in certain situations. It is possible to feel confused if you get hired to a new job. If the room is full of people sitting on their feet, with their feet up, they will likely give in to peer pressure. Regardless of whether you think these behaviors are unusual, you will follow the crowd. They must know what they're doing.

People naturally look at their peers to learn. This is simply our natural instinct as social animals, which can be used for the benefit of others. If you're trying to get people signed a petition, they will be more likely to sign it if there is a signature sheet with multiple signatures. The likelihood of getting more signatures is higher if you can get prominent or familiar names on the sheet.

People will ultimately defer to their peers rather than their superiors. You can adjust what others are doing by creating situations that allow you to do what you want.

Authority

While it is more common for people to follow peer pressure if they are confused or unsure of how to proceed, authority is probably the best way to convince someone. Because of how societies are built, people tend to trust authority. No matter what authority they are, there is always someone to defer to, be it a government, parent, boss, teacher or just someone who has more knowledge than you. A doctor is a great example for medical authority. While a lawyer is legal authority, a doctor would also be a great example. People will listen more to advice from authority figures if they are familiar with the credentials of the person, either by having them openly displayed or being introduced by someone else.

This can be very helpful in persuasion. It is possible to position yourself as an authority in any field you choose, even if it isn't your actual subject matter. Just by declaring that you are an authoritative source and offering proof of this, people will be more likely to listen to you. Although you may have a good knowledge of computers but not a degree, someone is more likely to listen to you if your answer is that you know how to fix and maintain computers. There are so many possibilities. Even if you only say that you've studied a subject at school, it might be enough to get them to believe your words.

Persuasion's benefits

Many benefits can be gained from being persuasive. Being able persuade others is an excellent trait. People who can legitimately persuade others, without using manipulation techniques or tricking people into doing something, are generally well-liked. They are both interested in the benefit of others, and they can achieve results that work well for all.

This results in happier individuals who can get at most a small portion of what they want. These happier individuals tend to be healthier, which leads to more benefits. This is a great way to make sure you are well-liked, happy, healthy, and successful.

Studying and mastering the art of persuasion has four main benefits. These are:

The instrumental function

The instrumental function simply means that by studying persuasion you will be able to use it more effectively. You can persuade better by understanding how you do it.

The knowledge- and awareness function

Knowledge and awareness refers to the idea of persuasion. The more you understand, the more informed you become and the more aware you will become. It is as easy as breathing. You can learn to persuade through practice and knowledge.

The defensive function

You can defend yourself by learning more about persuasion. Being acutely aware and able to defend yourself against persuasion will make you less susceptible.

The debunking feature

Finally, once mastering the three functions above, you can use your skills to see truth in situations even if they seem too good to true.

You will recognize the truth and not be influenced at all by lies.

Persuasion vs. Dark Persuasion

Having read all this information, you may now be curious about the difference between persuasion (or dark persuasion). While persuasion is a core part of both, dark persuasion is a different approach. Persuaders will more often be morally and ethically sound. They might persuade people into doing something that will end a war or create a new policy that will help everyone.

But dark persuaders are not blind to morality. They see what they want. The principles of persuasion help them to get it. They are open to doing the right things when they benefit, but they don't want to make sure the right thing is the right one. That is fine with them. They don't see why it would be a good idea to force the issue if it does not happen naturally. But as long as they're satisfied, everything is fine. If you're using dark persuasion then you should use the six principles. With the understanding that your needs are the most important thing to accomplish, each of these can be used with no hesitation. Perhaps you decide that you want your partner's ticket to a concert to be given up so that you can go with your friend. You are aware that your partner is looking forward to the concert and you realize that convincing them not to will be difficult, but you still want to do it anyway.

In order to make this happen, it would be a matter of using the principles for persuasion. You could go to great lengths to help your partner, offer to pay for their tickets, or point out other events you think your partner would enjoy on that particular night to appeal to scarcity. You can use any principle, but you must make it relevant for your partner. This will help you get the ticket, which he might eventually give you even though he is really eager to go. This is dark persuasion. Your partner did not feel the same way.

Chapter 3: Emotional Manipulation

Another type of manipulation that is possible and easily masterable is emotional manipulation. This form of manipulation allows people to take over in their own way. Someone who wants to control someone must be able to tap into their emotional states.

Emotional manipulation can be used to control people.

You'll be introduced to various topics about emotional manipulation as you go through this chapter. We will begin by discussing the meaning of emotions and why it is important. The next section will discuss the best emotions for manipulating, and the reasons why they work better than other emotions. Finaly, we'll wrap up by explaining what you would need to do if you wanted to manipulate others in this manner.

Next, we will look at the most effective emotions to manipulate others. There are many emotions you can manipulate and those are the ones most often targeted. This is why this book is so important. It will help you pay closer attention to what's happening around you and defend you against this type of manipulation.

We'll then discuss several ways you can be influenced and controlled by other people. Recognizing this will help you take greater control and know what to do to defend your rights.

The ability to manipulate emotions in others is very effective for those who need control. However, it can also cause a lot of harm to the person being controlled. Being able to understand and follow emotional manipulation will allow you to start to distance from it. You can stop yourself from becoming an accomplice to it by being able not to react to the signs. Remember that these people seek control. They want to influence others to get what their desire. Sometimes, these methods can even be brutal. They could inflict harm on others. They could leave people feeling hurt, sad, angry, or even shattered. They could make it difficult for them to have a healthy relationship. They are worth learning about.

Defining emotional manipulation

It all starts with a definition. It all starts with a definition. Emotional manipulation is a form that involves manipulating emotions. This is the main way one can influence others. People who use emotional manipulation are often manipulating others to get what they want. They deliberately and purposefully manipulate another person's emotions to obtain more control.

You might wonder, "Why are emotions so powerful?" Why is someone's emotional state so easy to control? The simple answer is that emotions are motivators. Emotions have the primary function of allowing you to manage and influence your life. They are your instincts. These emotions control how you respond.

Consider this: Being angry makes you more volatile. Anger makes it easier to provoke someone into attacking you. Anger means to feel defensive and need to protect yourself. Anger is the way your body responds when there are threats. This helps you to resolve difficult situations in a helpful way. Once you understand your emotions, you can control how someone reacts.

You can think about it. Knowing that an angry person will be more defensive in a situation is a good thing. You can use anger to cause someone to become more defensive. This is a common tactic to disintegrate groups. It can also be used to persuade two people into fighting. By knowing what they need, a manipulator could trigger one person to start an argument. That will cause everything to fall apart.

The manipulator must understand the emotions that we feel and the reasons they are there in order to be able influence them. They will be able to draw on these emotions whenever they need. For instance, you can ensure you trigger the right emotion to fulfill any purpose.

Knowing how emotions cause us think and act requires that we can understand what they trigger. A manipulator can simply identify the instincts that are triggered by emotions and when. After learning the causes of different reactions, they can start to force people to do what they want. They should be capable of identifying the emotions others may feel when they do certain things to them. These emotions can also help them identify which emotions will make it easier for them to get what they want. The universal emotions are the most commonly thought about emotions. A collection of emotions designed to keep you in line.

They work together with you to generate the additional effects that trigger what you need. There are seven emotions considered universal. This means that seven emotions have been shown to produce unique, clear results. These emotions can be understood and controlled by people.

Your emotions are important because they influence your behavior. You can communicate well by having these emotions. Your body language will change as you have them. You will be able to see the importance of your body language if you do it correctly. Your body language will reveal the emotions you are experiencing, which will be a focus of the book. But, it is the emotional body language that you use to describe what you do. Once you can understand your physical reactions to what you are doing, you will begin to see other people's emotional states. There are seven emotions that can be identified as universal. These emotions can be recognized based on body language, regardless of where you are in the world.

The following seven universal, motivating emotions can be used:

Happiness: It is vital to ensure that your behavior patterns are repeated. Happiness will give you the motivation to keep doing something. It is intended to reinforce your behaviour.

Sadness: A feeling of sadness that makes you want to avoid repeating something in the future. It is a sign that there was some type of loss or failure that caused this feeling of upset. If you see someone who you care about getting hurt, it could indicate that you are sad.

Anger: Anger can be used to inspire you to defend yourselves. When you feel fear or stress, anger is the result. It is there to protect.

Fear: Fear is the flight reaction or fight component. You feel fearful of something. It is an indication that you are being threatened. This is how you can effectively defend yourself. Only you need to be able to recognize what you are doing.

Disgust is a feeling that you have when you're exposed to something that isn't good for you. It is usually a visceral reaction. If you are exposed to something toxic, you will need to take steps to prevent it from happening again. You should avoid it to ensure that you don't get sickened.

Contempt can be described as a mixture of anger and hate. This is what you feel when something is truly offensive or bothersome for you. Contempt is when you perceive someone as being bad for yourself and are motivated to avoid them.

Surprise: A feeling of surprise that occurs when something does not go according to plan. Inducing a surprise reaction in another person can cause a situation in your life where you need to be attentive to them.

It takes an inborn understanding to be able control emotions. However, when you begin to understand your emotions and how they work, you can identify the ways things work. You can also start to notice patterns in order to protect yourself. For example, if you know that anger will cause your fights, then you can begin to see that someone is manipulating or trying to anger.

Emotional manipulation tactics

Let's now get to work. Let's take a look at the most common methods of manipulating others.

Knowing how to recognize them will allow you to start to protect yourself in the event that someone attempts to manipulate your life. You'll be able to protect yourself against these horrible tactics, which can be extremely dangerous, and you can rest assured that you're safe.

Into the FOG

Three key emotions will be instilled by the first tactic: Fear, obligation, guilt. Each of these feelings will cause intense reactions in others that will allow them to do what the manipulator asks. The manipulator must be close to their target in order to cause guilt or obligation. This is a difficult task. If there is no genuine interest in developing a relationship with another person, it can be difficult for them to reach out to you.

Fear can be used as a control tool to manipulate another person. The manipulator is afraid of harm and the other person feels they have to obey him.

Master emotional manipulators could tell their spouses, "If I try to take the kids, I will take them." This is to instill fear and cause them to obey.

A sense of obligation can be triggered by appealing to the target's level of responsibility. A sense of obligation is one that makes people do the right thing. Our families feel like we are obligated to them. We have a duty to look after them. This is another way of influencing someone to do what they want. Familial manipulators often use this tactic. They might whine, "It's my family!" You must help me!" in order to win.

The third type of guilt is one that appeals to unfulfilled obligations. We feel guilt when we don't complete an obligation. Someone might feel guilty if suddenly they realized they didn't complete something.

Love Bombing and Currency Devaluation

We'll then talk about love bombing, or devaluation. This involves making someone believe they are loved the most and then taking them off their pedestal to cause them to be in constant turmoil and instability. The other person will feel confused and out of balance if they are not sure what to expect. Through this cycle, the individual will feel that they must continue trying to bring about the positive effect they desire. But if they're not careful, the end result will create problems for everyone.

Love bombing and devaluation can lead to instability that is similar in nature to gambling. If someone becomes addicted to gambling or blind bags, they will continue to go back to the game even if it is not a good one. This creates a situation in that no matter how bad things get, the individual will try their best to stay in the relationship.

Intimidation

Another method of emotional manipulation that can be used is intimidation. Intimidation is a technique that allows a manipulator to control their target by making them feel fearful. If they make the target feel scared, they can also force them to follow their instructions. We'll be discussing intimidation as a type of body language in a future chapter. If they show another person the negative body language of another person, they should be able find that they are in control.

Malignant Sarcasm

Malignant Sarcasm is another type of emotional manipulation that can cause someone to react negatively. It is used to weaken the armor of the executioner, and chip away at their emotional self-esteem in order for the manipulator to maintain control.

The manipulator creates a situation in where the target feels like they are being poked, prodded or pushed at. If the target feels ripped apart and has to feel like their self-esteem is being destroyed, they will follow suit. But, they will also have to find a way of hiding what they are doing. The manipulator may disguise their words to others by using jokes. Think about the snide comments that a mother-inlaw might make to her daughter in law, for example by poking at their stomachs, or saying something like "When's the baby due?" If she becomes upset, it is best to say "It was just joke; why aren't you so offended?"

Chapter 4: Effective Reverse Psychology

BE AWARE OF YOUR PERSONALITY BEFORE APPLYING EVERSE PSYCHOLOGY

It is possible for some people to not answer the opposite psychology as well, as we have already mentioned. People who are open to following these guidelines may respond better. Some people are more resistant than others.

They are extremely intelligent and will do anything to get what they want. This person might be a candidate for reverse psychology.

Recall the conversations that you had with them. Are they more resistant than they are inclined to follow the flow of things? Consider a friend or relative who is an independent thinker who challenges the status quo. This person may be more vulnerable that an otherwise enjoyable person to reverse psychology.

Reverse psychology should be used with children if you are planning to use it. You will find that a child with a tendency to not work well together is more susceptible to reverse psychology than one who works well together.

UNCOMPLICATED EVERSE PSYCHOLOGY

Returnal psychology should be humorous and cheerful. This is especially true when it comes to young people. This is true. Use this technique to get someone to outswitch and cheat you.

Let's pretend that you are trying making your baby's bed. You might encourage her to wait until she brushes her teeth to make sure she isn't feeling obliged to help you make her bed. It's likely that you will see him making his bed in the next room. This is his way for you to see that he can care for himself.

If you are dealing with an adult, this technique might also apply. You can allow the person to think they have the truth. You can choose from a foreign movie that has substitutes, or one that is comedy-based.

You are looking to watch a foreign film. A simple example of this is "I don't believe my patience can hold me over for subtitles." It's a shock to discover that your buddy has chosen the humor for the foreign film to demonstrate that the focus is higher.

WHAT DO YOU WANT FROM THE OTHER PERSON

Before you make any decisions about reverse psychology or what kind of usage to use, consider the wishes of the other person. Sometimes, it may be necessary to use a more complicated form of reverse psychology. The level of resistance that anyone has to overcome in order to succeed at anything is beyond what conventional reverse psychology might allow.

You might be in a difficult area and your friend wants to go to a music concert. Reverse psychology can work, even though it might seem terrible. Just say, "You're right." You should get up. You should. He says, "You live only once." This is something he fully supports as he wants to be there.

Don't try to argue against your self in these circumstances. Say something like, "It is your decision. You must decide what to do. This area is hazardous, I'm sure. The only thing you can do is decide what's best for yourself.

Your friend can have a peek here. If your friend is normally resistant to your advice, he might be willing to listen instead of resisting it. He might choose not to travel to the town due to the risk.

FOCUS ONE OBJECTIVE

Always keep your focus on the things you want them to do. Sometimes, there might be disputes when reverse psychology is used. You could easily get sidetracked by an argument. Take a note of your preferred outcome and try to remember it.

SUGGESTIONS

One suggestion is for the therapist to guide the client to react to ideas to change subjective experiences, perceptual emotional thinking or behavioural changes using hypnosis.

The suggestion is what fascinates hypnotic effect. One example is that a person can feel calm and concentrated when they are hypnotized while holding a wound to their arm. The only way to feel pain relief is when you suggest that your arm become bumbled and sensitive. The same is true of other types.

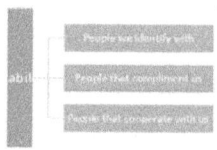

The proposals can be either direct or indirect. "You may be able to sense changes in your arm's sensing," as an example. One idea is that propositions alter our expectations of what might happen. We then get experiences that suit our needs.

TYPES HYPONOTIC SUGGESTIONS

Direct

Direct hypnotic propositions are those that are immediately obvious to the customer. They're not vague nor mysterious. They are not meant for the customer to think. They are easy and straightforward. The best example of a simple suggestion is "Walk 15 minutes per day to feel energetic and happy."

Indirect

Indirect notions in hypnosis tend to be less accurate, more unclear, and can take many forms. This is a great example: "Since arriving on this planet, there have been many challenges in your life. That's quite excellent for you. I know there's a remedy, maybe in the deeper portion of your ideas for this issue. I ask if that will happen in the session sooner than later.

Effective Hypnotic Suggestions

Straightforward

Hypnotic propositions should be clear and concise. The brain is brilliant. Keep it short and to-the-point. It makes the intellect more understandable.

Practical

The hypnotizing idea should ask customers to do more than one thing. It is practical to the suggestion. The intellect is capable understanding. This proposal should therefore be easy to comprehend.

Present Tense

Never use the tense futur. You can use the phrase "I do twenties," instead of "I'm gonna do twenty push-ups," to illustrate. The future is in the future. This is how the subconscious mind interprets the term "will". Hypnotic proposals that use the present tense are not as effective.

Believable

Your proposal must be realistic. It is wrong to suggest hypnosis and claim that your arm will grow overnight. However, customers should be pushed out of their comfort zone. It is the job and responsibility of the hypnotists to give credible recommendations. It builds customer loyalty.

Be positive

Instead of worrying about what isn't desired, suggestive words should emphasize the positive. An example of this might be "I don't really wish to be this worried" or "I feel calmer. The spirit is well guided. Everything we focus on is growing, so the suggestion must be positive. This is how the brain functions.

Reward

You should link the reward to your proposal. It could be, for example, that I spend thirty minutes per day practicing my yoga and I feel peaceful and calm. The brain functions best when there are positive feedback loops. The best prize is the one that is inherent to the work. Walking is an amazing experience. The weight loss for an intrinsic prize isn't noticeable and will be not measured.

Measurable

If they succeed, the person will be able to see how many measurable suggestions are made. This is an example of a measurable suggestion: "I do 20 push ups every morning, and I am invigorated." It is enjoyable for the mind to be successful. A great therapist provides rewards to customers that show customer satisfaction.

Suggestions to Improve Our Daily Life

The phenomena of suggestibility isn't just applicable to hypnotic situations. In order to do the indicated things, there are many instances where people have been manipulated to a large extent. One example of this is a bank "Enter". It is a simple idea. A simple idea like "High Voltage," however is not that straightforward. It isn't as clear-cut as it seems. Because the sign for "High Voltage," doesn't presume anyone knows anything about electricity, it shouldn't be so confusing. He actually says, "Be cautious, this can be dangerous", "Stay away", and "you might get hurt."

In some instances, the ideas might be even more delicate. What about going to an ATM where there was no one working? The queue at the withdrawal counter will likely be the first thing to welcome you. This is not a casual gesture. You will naturally go up to the machine and withdraw the money. You're either joining the line or leaving. You basically get the hint when arriving without it being mentioned elsewhere: wait your turn, fella or leave if that's not possible.

Convention plays a major part in our experience with most activities (as a widely recognized habit in society). How we perceive things and how they are perceived is the basis of our previous experience. It's not surprising that you gave him an amount more than enough to settle your account. After handing him a $ 5.15 note, he says, "Did the fifteen cent?" It's clear that his inquiry only focuses on one thing. He wants to give you the balance, but he's not giving enough. It is possible to extend the idea further by leaving him the change or paying for your ride in the exact amount.

Another example would be "This is your way please." There is a term that five-star hotels are familiar with. You are likely to have never met this person before. Follow them without asking questions. On one hand, it is your protection. It's an actual fact. You must have witnessed enough crime for you to understand that it's not wise to follow strangers. You wouldn't do it in another place (e.g. dark alley). However, you have had prior experiences that lead to the notion and are certain that this stranger is associated the facility. As you hear, "Pease. I will accompany you to your chamber.

It is important to consider contexts when interpreting suggestibility. Interpreting the suggestions depends on many aspects: tone, atmosphere, weather conditions, dressing style, time of the day, age, perception, presentation and condition of the self.

Noting that the platform for extreme may contain ideas is a good idea. Some proposals may be so radical that they exceed the credibility bar, but they are presented with a strong tone. They are also updated with achievable criteria. Most people will accept that such an "assertion", unless it is true, is made.

It is not just about the outcome of the proposal. The suggestions might seem hopeless. A young, unemployed graduate will most likely accept the suggestion of a dream position if he provides a certain amount. This is how scammers operate. They combine extreme and despair.

Some Effective Tips

It is important to remember that ideas should not be just a proposition or a factual assertion that the individual seeking the advice wishes to hear. It must be credible, regardless of whether it is presented in real-life situations or in hypnosis sessions. The individual should believe and want to believe what is being presented.

Sometimes, selling you a vehicle or a product is easy for a salesman. Although he doesn't know you, he can see the potential. It's because you are there. He will make you an offer of information as you travel through the dealership.

The vendor informs the buyer that the price for your automobile will rise in a few weeks, but that he can sell it to you at the current price. He goes on to detail the functions of the automobile, and why it's a limited edition.

You might not get a special edition, a longer lasting engine or extended guarantee. It is possible that the salesman will recommend you buy the car.

However, he is only able to suggest possible solutions. He has to decide if you want to purchase the automobile, or if it is not available anymore. This proposal will ensure that you spend your money. The remarks of his father struck a chord with a family because they want to buy the car.

A few words that will help you make your suggestion effective

The words can be convincing in hypnosis sessions as well as in daily life.

Because

Its name, "cause", makes it quite powerful. It is easy to use and conceal its existence. The unconscious mind uses the word "for" to give it a reason. It is fair, reasonable, attractive, and practically incontrovertible.

Miracle & Strange

Talking to someone immediately with "I wonder", "I'm curious" or "I have a question" can trigger an unconscious reaction.

Imagine

The psychological image that the word "imagine" creates is what it means. If a salesperson, therapist or inscription uses the word, they aim to generate a mental illustration. To this effect, your brain will respond quickly by trying to do the exact same thing.

Your name/you

It has a powerful effect on you. It is said that no one has something more wonderful than the sound of their own name. We are always interested when we hear it.

The Further

As you discover more about hypnosis power and power, you'll be more fascinated by this book. "The more" can be a powerful phrase in hypnosis that causes your mind to produce a reaction. It's quite like "As."

As

"Listen to the sound of my voice . This is a typical line for hypnotherapy. Its purpose? To relax and concentrate your attention. It's like "The More."

Tamper or just Tamper

"Pretend", a hypnotic phrase that means "imagine," is the hypnotic word for "pretend". It is used to incite subconscious thought. "Always pretend you are relaxed. You will be surprised at how big it feels." "Pretending" does not remove the customer's demand for impeccable work. Assume that you are right. Maybe you'll soon start doing it properly.

The Value of Well-Designed Suggestions

It is important that you are able to comprehend the importance of well-crafted propositions in hypnotherapy. This article will provide guidelines for preparing high-quality proposals.

Complexity is avoided

Since the subconscious works literarily and requires you to speak correctly, it is important to use proper grammar. You shouldn't declare: "They will be soft and fluffy when your head touches the cushion." Although this may sound like a straightforward statement, your subconscious might wonder if the cushion is actually a fluffy, soft head.

Positive sentence

You need to be aware of negative terms, especially those that are powerful and can transmit impossible messages. You can abstractly use negative words, even though they may seem inevitable in some cases. You could say, "It is not necessary to cheat anymore." Here is the abstract of "not more."

Strengthen Interest

Any suggestion for hypnotherapy should get strong attention. If the target audience isn't interested, the proposal may not be successful. It must express the wishes of the individual.

Create emotional existence

If the hypnotic ideas need to be approved, emotion is essential. Hypnotists can use positive emotions, which they can achieve through images and videos that provide the individual with pleasure.

Don't create deliberate objections

It is highly likely that we will reject a recommendation made against the wishes or needs of a person. It is more likely we will not ignore the conscious vital faculties. We are careful to ensure that our ideas do not contain any unpleasant aspects.

Chapter 5: Recognize A Manipulator

Characteristics and functions of a manipulator

Every manipulator has certain personality traits that help them control people, situations, or actions.

Self-Protection

Manipulative individuals are driven by self-protection. To protect themselves, they will engage. Some manipulators don't realize that they have skills. It is their self-protection and instinctive need to manipulate others that drives them.

You can view self-protection and manipulation as motives. Every manipulator does a bad thing, self-protection becomes the valid reason. It is all about their feelings and motives. It is a way for manipulators to manipulate people's emotions.

While every human being is born with the instinct of self-protection and manipulation, not all people are able to use it effectively. A manipulative mind is born out of a strong desire to protect ones self-motives. This creates a dangerous, manipulative personality. Because manipulators have such a strong belief in their actions, they are able to easily justify their bad choices. They can give an amazing explanation for something that is totally absurd.

No Regards for Personal Space

Although manipulators may not be aware that they are manipulators, they lack the understanding of one's personal identity. The flip side is that manipulators who are intent on manipulating people don't give a damn about their personal space. A manipulator targets people emotionally, physically and spiritually. They may attack one aspect of your identity or all aspects.

If the victim is subject to forceful manipulation, they may experience different stages or exhaustion. Abusers, intimidators, or other direct manipulators weaken victims and devalue personal space.

But subtle manipulation is more dangerous. The manipulator starts to control the victim's thoughts and behavior, but the victim is unaware. The realization period happens after the manipulator leaves your personal space. People feel angry, remorseful or other hurtful feelings.

People's personal spaces are the work space for manipulators. They will only be able to harm their victims by learning the details of their personal space. The ability to read the identity of people is what makes manipulators so powerful. Before manipulating others, they examine their mental, physical, and emotional capabilities.

If you asked a manipulator about their personal space, they would respond, "It doesn't matter if you live apart." People reveal their identities through words and actions. "So, what is personal identity? A manipulator believes in opening every door that can be opened to gain information about their victims. It's how they feel about entering into the victim's psychology to observe.

Self-Confidence

A manipulative individual is always confident about their actions, thoughts, and behavior. However they may show or hide this confidence when they wish. They can avoid taking responsibility. They would rather have other people take the blame. They can blame others for their actions, which is how manipulators work. They may work behind the scenes, but they come out looking confident if it helps them. If their purpose is to take responsibility, manipulators are willing to speak up.

Manipulators are confident, but they don't leave any room for their victim to survive. To make their victim feel real, manipulators conceal their confidence. The manipulator on the other side, however, shows maximum confidence when using intimidation or sarcasm to manipulate.

On two different days, you can hear the same person speak two different things.

"I don't know how I should handle my money." Can we open a shared account?

"I decide how my money is spent, how I shop, where I travel, and what clothes to wear. You can't control me.

The manipulator may manipulate the confidence levels of others, but it is not possible to change their inner world. This person has been self-confident about their abilities since childhood. Self-confidence is not something that they possess. An manipulator's true trait is their ability to display or hide confidence.

Motivator

Manipulators can be used to motivate others. The manipulators' strong communication skills enable them to tell victims what they want. Manipulators know how to read a person's emotions and sensitivities. This helps them understand how caring, kind or practical an individual is. The manipulators then motivate the person they are trying to target. For instance, a manipulator could praise someone's facial features, especially if they are self-conscious about their appearance.

"You have a lovely smile, and your caring personality makes that smile even more beautiful to my face."

If they have a good understanding of the insecurities of someone, they will praise them subtly by giving specific compliments. These lies can be easily bought by the victim.

Practical empathy

Empathy is the ability of understanding others' feelings and sharing them with them. A manipulator does not feel general empathy. Manipulators can sense empathy in a practical way. They are able to understand and share people's emotions without sharing their feelings. A manipulator looks at a person's happy or sad face. Although the emotions are clearly visible, manipulators can actually see them and use that information to help them achieve their goals.

Talking to a manipulator about relationships will show that they tend to break down relationships into wants, needs, and practical aspects. They will give you reasons two people are in love. A manipulator would tell you that if two celebrities marry, it is because one is trying to climb the ladder, while the other is just trying over an old relationship.

Manipulative individuals see the dynamics in relationships. They can spot intrigue, jealousy rivalry affection, attraction hope, need, and rivalry. They manipulate these dynamics to ruin harmony between people. They can encourage or discourage your feelings of love and hate. It all depends what their big plan includes.

Hidden Insecurities

Behind all the charm and confidence lies an insecure person. They can observe their emotions and understand their insecurities.

But, like their self-confidence they can hide their insecurities. A manipulator can be seen victimizing himself. There is some truth in that. They manipulate their insecurities to create a character that fools people.

Sometimes manipulators can be driven by insecurity to manipulate vulnerable people. They want to be seen and be admired, but they cannot do that unless they find someone more vulnerable than their own. This is how the search for vulnerable victims begins, and many people end up being hurt.

An manipulator is a person with insecure personality traits that makes them obsessive towards their goals. Insecure, manipulative people will look for reasons to blame their partner when they hear their apologies. Manipulators desire their victims to follow in their footsteps. Some manipulators are motivated to give praises, others want to exert control over their victims. You should also be aware that motives can vary from victim to victim.

Multiple personalities

Manipulators act like chameleons. Their ability to adapt to changing situations or people is what makes them manipulators. Many personality traits are present in every person. But manipulators know that not everyone hides them or displays them to gain something. They manipulate themselves to create a fake persona for a victim. You will never see them laughing at you or casually talking to you if they want you to be scared. It is part of their constant character play. It is easy to believe that your boss or partner can be very serious and intimidating, but they behave totally differently in different situations.

Manipulators' ability to alter personalities is dangerous. It is easy to make a mental picture of friends or partners when we are in relationships. But, what if that picture is incorrect? The perfect partner is right in front you. But they're cheating and getting away.

Three aspects are important when manipulators try to change people's personalities. They focus on their behavior, opinions, as well as their feelings. They will choose to behave a certain way before certain people. To gain trust they mix righteousness into their behavior. Manipulators are able to manipulate their victims using multiple behavior patterns on random days. For control, manipulative spouses may switch their moods frequently to keep their partner under control.

Manipulators have the ability to debate for and against both sides at once. They are unable to give specific opinions and can be held accountable by no one. It allows them to switch sides and present opinions, allowing them to say what the victim wants. They can make it seem like two victims are talking to one manipulator at the exact same time. To reap the benefits of both sides, it's important to be open-minded.

Indirect Communication

Although manipulators are good communicators they also like to use others to express their ideas. They may present themselves to be straightforward and just say what they think, but they also like to plant seeds inside people's heads. You will not realize they are manipulating you. They make you believe that their ideas and your ideas are yours. If you do, it's your fault. You came alone."

Jealousy

Though manipulators will not admit it to themselves, jealousy is a large part of their mindset. It is the driving force that drives many manipulators to exploit other people's vulnerabilities. It can be triggered by almost anything. Because manipulators are driven to feel superior, manipulators may feel jealous about their spouses, parents, siblings, and other friends. The jealousy does not stop until they can control the person. They can manipulate people's emotions and their actions to feel more powerful than the others.

Self-Centered

All characteristics boil down to this single idea. Manipulators have a tendency to be self-centered. They don't understand or care about others' thoughts, lives, emotions, or mental states. They only care what they want. They are not responsible for the consequences of people being hurt, whether it be physically, emotionally, or mentally. If the manipulator has a good reason to make people disposable, they will consider them expendable. This is how a manipulator perceives the world. It doesn't matter how charming, caring, and logical they sound. They don't mean a single thing. It's all a carefully crafted combination of words and emotions that manipulate people and situations.

Chapter 6: Psychology Of Persuasion, Manipulation

People struggle often to recognize the difference between manipulations and persuasion. Because they are trying to persuade each other to do something different, it is obvious that they want the same thing.

They do have some key differences. Manipulation, for example, is focused on manipulating the victim, while persuasion focuses more on the needs and interests of the recipient.

The most important distinction between the two is the fact that manipulation seeks the benefit of the manipulator, and persuasion the benefit of the persuader.

Do you recall how intention is crucial when using dark psychology to your advantage?

This is perhaps the most obvious example of this being the truth.

Manipulation vs. Persuasion

Before you compare the two, first learn what manipulation and persuasion mean. For a better understanding of how the two are different, you can take a closer look to each definition.

PERSUASION

At its core, persuasion means convincing others to do things that are contrary to their gut reactions. Although it changes someone's mind it can also be used to benefit the persuader. Although there are some instances where the persuader can benefit from the other person's changing of mind, the general principle is one of kindness and generosity.

This can be done either outwardly to change the minds of others or inwardly for oneself to alter their behavior.

The four main elements of persuasion are essential to make it effective. It involves persuading someone else, a message that is being persuaded, a target for persuasion, as well as a context within which the persuasion is heard.

These four items are essential for persuasive communication.

MANIPULATION

However, manipulation is more like persuasion. But with an added element. The process of manipulation is often disguised. It is intentionally deceitful and dishonest. This makes it inherently untrustworthy.

The manipulator will only look out for his best interests, and he won't care about lying to get the results he wants. That is why he is actively manipulating. He wants what he wants even if it means forcing the point.

The manipulator is motivated by his selfishness. He would rather improve his situation than help others, and he will do this at any cost. Manipulation, which is often abusive in nature, can sometimes inflicts injury. But the manipulator cares not. It doesn't really matter if people get hurt, as long as the manipulator has what he wants.

Are you familiar Machiavellianism

That is again where the power of manipulation comes into play. The ends justify all the means, and this is all the manipulator has to justify the manipulation.

Three elements are necessary for manipulation to occur. It is important to conceal the intent and manipulative behaviors at the beginning so that the victim does not perceive them as friendliness. To gain control and an advantage, the manipulator must have a clear understanding of the victim's vulnerabilities. The manipulator must also not be concerned about any harm done.

In the end, manipulation comes in many forms. These can include gas lighting or playing the victim. They all leave the victim confused and upset.

Manipulation, which this book does not condone, is something that you should avoid due to it's more negative and dark nature. However, you can still use it at your own risk. You might not like the results.

The Key Differences

These two things may appear very similar but you can easily tell the difference with just three questions. If you ask these questions and understand your answers, it is possible to determine if your attempts at convincing someone to do another thing are persuasive or manipulative.

These three questions can be answered:

What are you trying to persuade the other person?

Are you completely truthful and forthright?

How does this benefit the other person

These questions show the difference. Persuaders are able to explain that they want to persuade. Persuaders should be open and honest with their counterparts. They want the other person feel that they can persuade them.

A manipulator will most likely say they are doing it to benefit themselves, and they may even withhold information.

Did you see the example of a car in which intention matters? It is manipulative to push someone to purchase the car in order to get a higher commission. If you're pushing someone to buy the car simply because it seems like a good fit, you are persuasive.

Principles of Persuasion

Six principles apply to persuasion. These six principles can help you convince someone else to do what your want.

When you apply these principles, it is much easier to convince another person. This is because you are using the human mind's workings and setting up the conditions for the other person to do what you want.

These six principles may be used in different ways but they all help to create the right environment for persuasion. Different results will be achieved if you appeal each of the six principles. While not everyone will be able to agree with each principle, it is almost impossible to identify the least useful one against someone else.

RECIPROCITY

Reciprocity describes the obligation people feel to reciprocate for something done. Reciprocity refers to the obligation you feel when someone does good things for you.

As an example, if someone presents you with a birthday present, they will make you feel like you must give them the same gift when your birthday comes around. This can be extremely useful in convincing people. To get someone to do something, you just need to make them feel indebted to your efforts to motivate them.

Are you conscious of how empathy encourages people into selfless behaviour and that survival often comes from selfless behaviors?

Yes, that was persuasion. This is probably the most compelling and persuasive principle because it relies on obligation. And with obligation comes guilt. The feeling of guilt is accompanied by the desire to be free from the feeling.

This is a common way that they can be used against your in a variety ways. Hotel staff may offer complimentary water, while flight attendants may provide refreshment. This is to indebt them. You will feel more likely take care of the place you're in, no matter if it's a hotel or on an airplane. You might also notice this with waiters. How many times have you had a fortune cookie mint, chocolate, or chocolate delivered back to you along with your receipt? This encourages tipping.

This can be very useful. If you are looking for something, ask someone to do it first.

If you are able to ask for what they can do to help, they will more likely be willing to help you in return. This principle is something the most successful leaders are familiar with: they will always ask the people around them how they can assist them. If they do, they will find that others will follow their lead.

AUTHORITY

According to scientists, people listen more to people who state the truth without verifying it. This is because they believe the person is an authority.

This is true?

No, not really. People are more likely to accept something when it comes from someone they consider to be an authority on the subject. It is obvious that you have accepted the sentence without thinking twice about it. A person who regards an individual as an authority will be more inclined to trust an authority when they claim something about the subject matter he or she is an expert in.

People will often take advice from dietitians about diets more readily than they would from a veterinarian.

This can be leveraged to your advantage. Make yourself the authority and advocate for what you are trying convince others to do. It is important to make sure that anyone you hire to help you buy a car knows what you are talking.

If you want someone to trust your advice in a relationship, they can listen to what you did in the past to get exactly the results that you desired.

People prefer to listen to someone who has more experience with a particular situation than to do whatever seems to make sense.

LIKABILITY

One of the most basic principles is likability. This refers to the person being persuaded's liking for the persuader. People will follow through more if someone they love asks them to do something.

Would you rather do something you dislike for your best friends or something you love for your enemy?

It is likely that you will do more for your friend than you would for yourself, even if you don't like it. This is because people naturally want help others they like.

What then makes someone relatable?

It is simple. It all comes down to three points.

Three traits are necessary to determine if someone is trustworthy: They must be approachable and open to learning from you.

Think back to the last occasion you visited a car dealer, other salesperson's offices or areas of selling. Perhaps they shared their own story to make it relatable.

If you learn something random about someone, it is easier to identify them as an individual with a life, rather than just a nameless, faceless stranger. When you get to know the other person better, it's easier to relate.

The other person may compliment you and tell you how funny you are.

Lastly, the salesperson might say something along lines of "Help Me Help You." This creates a kind of camaraderie -- suddenly, you are all working towards the same goal. Each of you will have to find you the perfect product.

SCARCITY

Scarcity can only be described as supply and demande. Therefore, things in high demand are not valuable and no one wants. If everyone has it easily, they're no longer desirable.

However, when something becomes scarce, people begin to see the value in it.

You are looking for a limited-edition game console

It is worth the extra cost because there are only limited quantities available. Or at least that is what the person paying extra for it might tell himself. In reality, scarcity is deliberately created.

The console could have been made in unlimited numbers by the gaming company, but they decided to not increase the demand and interest. By doing this, they can drive up demand and thus convince more people who are interested to buy the products that are produced. For those who already own a console, they may choose to purchase another in limited edition.

This can be used in many other ways. It is possible to be unique in a relationship by stating that you are with someone.

You are the only one who is out there, no matter how many fish there may be. That means you have the power to leverage your partner's insecurity and remind them that they are worth their time and that you are worthy of being there.

To use scarcity as a principle you must place some limitation. You should make sure that the deal has an expiration date and time. Also, remind the other person of the consequences if they cancel the deal. This will help you convince the other person to take action on what you have requested without too much effort.

If the other person feels they will lose out on a deal or something that is truly special, they will be more inclined to accept it.

Social proof

Social proof, in its simplest form, is just peer pressure. People feel more pressured when their peers do the same as them -- even when they have to comply with their authority.

People have a natural desire for belonging. The easiest way to fulfill that desire is to follow what others are doing. By doing this, everyone will see you as part of the group.

Because people are naturally inclined to like others, they can often be persuaded into following a behavior or taking an action by seeing other people doing the same thing.

To illustrate, if you want someone else to buy your item, introduce them to someone that is like them. They will be more likely than others to purchase the item if they are able to identify with it.

This is very useful to have if you are in a leadership capacity. You just need to make sure that everyone else follows your lead. If everyone functions well together, newcomers can easily blend in.

Use this tool to sell your items. You should target your ads so that people in your target market enjoy the item you are selling.

To encourage your child's commitment to a particular behavior, show them other children doing it. When they see others doing something, people are more likely to follow suit.

Consistency & commitment

People are drawn to consistency. This is because consistency is something society intrinsically values. It is predictable, reliable, and familiar. It makes it easy for everyone to predict how the situation will unfold.

People like the familiar, so they are more likely to choose the familiar.

Encouragement of a commitment can help you to do this. This is because people want to be trusted and have a positive outlook.

If you want to appeal more to consistency and committment, you must first convince the other person of some kind. Ask them to do something small, like shredding some documents from your files while the other person's is in the back.

You can use this method to gradually convince the other person you are doing more for them, asking them to do additional tasks while they shred your documents. Because the other person has already committed to shredding your documents, it is more likely that the other person will agree to take your garbage with them while you are gone.

Slowly but surely you make more requests, until the other person has done a fair bit of work that he/she probably wouldn't have accepted to do if they had been more open to your request.

Make use of the principles for persuasion

You must first understand the purpose of these principles.

To achieve your desired results, you can use each one in different situations. Are you trying sell a car You might want to leverage scarcity and likability to get the result you desire.

Are you able to convince someone else to run an errand on your behalf?

You are more likely to succeed in this situation if your appeals to likability, reciprocity and trustworthiness.

It will be up to you ultimately to choose which of these principles is the most appropriate to help you achieve your desired outcome.

Chapter 7: How Do You Know If Someone Is Manipulating Your Emotions? And Tips To Escape From Toxic Relationships Or People

Toxicity is a form of mold that grows over time. If you aren't careful, it could spread to you. Consider this: If you ever had a small pint of raspberries that looked mostly good but one was looking a bit fuzzy, you will know how important it is to get rid of the toxic portion. You should remove it as soon as possible. Otherwise, mold could spread to your perfectly healthy raspberries. This is a major problem. To ensure that your raspberries don't go bad, it's important to remove any moldy ones. Moldy relationships in your life can lead to trouble.

What is a toxic relationship?

Toxic relationships are those which are unhealthy. They have destructive or toxic behaviors that are very harmful. It is toxic relationships in your life that cause you pain. They make you feel terrible, both physically and psychologically. Toxic relationships can cause you to lose everything that makes a relationship strong: trust. You lack respect. You lack compassion. This is a major problem for both you and your partner.

Most likely, the toxic person doesn't know that they are toxic. Because of their dysfunctional upbringing, they often have already been diagnosed. Sometimes they are not aware of their tendencies. Some people may be able to work through their issues with therapy, and they might want to make a change. Whatever the reason, it is essential to end the toxic relationship.

In most people's lives, toxic relationships are the main source of stress. It can be difficult to recognize who is toxic and how they are bringing you down.

Dealing with toxic people

Five things are required to deal with toxic individuals in your life. Each one is listed below.

1. Identify People at Risk

Understanding your problem is the first step towards solving it. They might be watching over you, just like a bird of Prey, waiting to grab its victim. Or, they may already have you in their grips and you don't know it. Whatever the case may be you should identify those involved.

2. Build your self-esteem

Other people must see you as a human being, just like them. They need to view you as being full of value, dignity, honour. They should consider you worthy of acknowledgment by others. You can't expect others to appreciate your self-worth and selfesteem if you don't.

3. Effective Communication

You are now able identify certain people as toxic. You are now able to identify specific traits associated with toxicity. You are now aware that Chloe can be negative towards you. Charlie's lies can certainly make the devils blush. John's desire and ability to dominate is what caused his threats against you weeks ago. All of these are now fully understood by you. What's next?

4. A Mediator is a good choice

It is possible to involve a third party where necessary. But they are not coming to your aid to judge you. They aren't pointing fingers; they facilitate effective communication between the two of you.

5. Responsibilities

You could provoke another person's behavior. You know what toxic traits are. These traits are what make you believe you are not toxic. Is it because you think you're perfect? You might not be able communicate your reservations to others effectively.

A toxic relationship must be ended

The "when" is before the "how", which makes sense. If you believe you have to eliminate toxic people from your life each time you recognize them, you are wrong. Yes, it is possible to still learn how to deal toxic people. As usual, my style will be concise, specific, and practical.

When to quit

First, know when it's time to end a relationship. This happens when the relationship is irretrievably ended. You might be promised a better outcome, but you will get worse if you give them another chance.

How to end an abusive relationship

Two situations are important and you need to know how to handle them. Both of these situations are affected by how close you are with the other person.

For Close Relatives

Close relatives include your parents, siblings, in-laws, cousins, spouse, etc. In this situation, you can keep the bond that binds your family and still distance yourself from the person. Assuming that it is your parents you will have figured out who is toxic to you. The parental bond should never be severed. This is in gratitude for all that our parents have done.

You must keep your distance and not allow them to influence you or interfere in the affairs of your life. You can always drop in to check on them, their health, and how they are doing. However, you should never allow them to have any influence over your decisions. If they attempt to influence you, stop them. If they don't, politely excuse themselves.

When it comes to your spouse's case, you need to be cautious and slow down, especially when children are involved. There is a reason why it is a "for-better-or-for-worse" affair. It is necessary to persist a little longer. Consider the effects of a divorce upon your kids' upbringing. Don't rush. This is why I recommend marriage counselling first.

Be sure to communicate the idea of therapy to your partner. Let them know that you are thinking about your marriage and your children. It is a good idea to offer to pay for the financial costs if you can. You can also look into other methods, such a mentor shared or any mediator, if therapy fails. If your attempts to repair things fail, you might consider other options such as a mentor or mediator. You may be better off taking care of them when you're not there. Other people have achieved this success, and you can too.

For Non-Relatives

This category includes your boss and colleagues, your fiance(e), girlfriend, boyfriend, etc. For your fiancee, it is likely that you will need to split up. You can't be together if your relationship is toxic. For your friends, it's time to end any relationships. Let them know about your decision and the reasons behind it. Communicate effectively. Example:

"Chloe. It is true that you do remember our conversation at Point Cafe last October. Your promise to change was broken, but I doubt it. I can name two instances when you have done exactly the same thing you said you would. I made it clear that I do not want friends who don't respect me. It seems that we will both be more successful if we work together. I am not trying to argue. I am only expressing my decision. May the odds favor us. Thank you for the great time.

It is important to let your colleagues or coworkers know that you will still have a professional relationship, but not in any other capacity.

Chapter 8: Mindwashing

Coercive Persuasion also known as Brainwashing, is a system of convincing nonbelievers to agree to a particular command, allegiance or doctrine. An informal term for any technique used to manipulate the thoughts or actions of people against their will, desires, or knowledge. In order to control the environment both physically and socially, the goal is to break down loyalties to those groups or individuals that are not favorable to the individual. To show the individual his wrong thinking patterns and encourage loyalty, the leader must also be followed.

This term is used most often to refer to a program that involves ideological remolding, or indoctrination. The most common techniques for brainwashing involve being isolated from former associates and information sources; a rigorous regimen that requires absolute obedience. There are also strong social pressures to cooperate and rewards for it. Physical and psychological punishments can be used for non-cooperation, including social ostracism.

The nature of brainwashing, as it took place in communist prisons, was widely discussed after the Chinese Communist victory (1949) and after the Korean War and Vietnam wars. In recent years, it has been reported that brainwashing is used to infringe religious and political cults. This has prompted concern in the United States.

Deprogramming, or the reverse of brainwashing, is a method that involves intensive psychotherapy and confrontation. This has proven quite successful with religious cult members.

The degree and duration of changes in attitude or points of view will depend on the personality and motivation of the individual and how supportive the environment is.

The study of brainwashing in psychology, also known as thought Reform, falls within the scope of "social Influence." Social influence occurs every minute of every single day. It's the accumulation of all possible ways that people can influence their beliefs, attitudes, and behavior. For example, the compliance method is designed to effect a change in behavior. It does not care about beliefs or attitudes. It is the "Just do what you want" approach. Persuasion, on the other hand, aims for a change in attitude, or "Do it because it'll make you feel good/happy/healthy/successful." The education method, also known as the "propaganda technique" when you don't believe the information being taught, aims for social-influence gold. It attempts to alter a person's beliefs. Brainwashing can be a severe form social influence. It combines all of the above to make a person think differently, sometimes against his will.

Brainwashing can be a highly intrusive form or influence. Therefore, the subject must be isolated from the outside world and made dependent. You often hear about brainwashing happening in prison camps and totalist cults. The brainwasher (the agent), must have complete control of the target (the person being brainwashed). Therefore, the agent's will dictates how the victim should sleep, eat, use the toilet, and fulfill other basic human requirements. The brainwasher breaks down the target's identity so that it no longer works. The agent then replaces it by another set of beliefs, attitudes, or behaviors that work in the target's current environment.

While psychologists generally believe that brainwashing could be possible, there are some who think it is unlikely or more severe than the media portrays. Brainwashing may be defined as the threat or occurrence of physical harm. Most extremist cults are not allowed to practice true brainwashing as they don't physically abuse recruits. Some definitions use "nonphysical force and control" to assert their influence. Experts agree that the brainwashing process is rarely permanent, regardless of how it is defined. It does not eliminate the victim's previous identity. However, the victim will be in hiding until the "new identities" are stopped being reinforced.

Some psychologists believe the apparent conversion of American prisoner of war prisoners during the Korean War was due simply to torture and not brainwashing. And most POWs captured in the Korean War didn't convert to communism. Which raises questions about reliability. Does brainwashing work across cultures and personalities? Or is it dependent on the target being susceptible to influence? Next, we will look at the brainwashing process as described by one expert. We will also learn what makes a target easy to influence.

It's time to let go of your self

The first stage of brainwashing involves the breakdown of the self. To make the subject more open to receiving the desired identity, the agent will want to dissolve their old identity. This step is vital to continue the process. If the subject holds on to their old identity and is not willing to change, they will not be able achieve their goals. The first step to changing an identity is to break it down and make the subject think about what's happening around them. This involves several steps that include assault on the subject's identity and self-betrayal.

Assault on Identity

The systematic attack against the identity of the subject or their sense of self is called the assault on their identity. It involves the systematic attack of their core system and belief systems as well their ego. It forces the subject to question their identity, making them question everything they've ever known. The agent will spend considerable time denigrating everything the subject is. For example, an agent in prisoner camp will tell the subject things like "You do not defend freedom," "You cannot be a man," or "You can't be a soldier" for days to months. This is done so the subjects become disoriented and confused. This will cause the subject to lose their belief system and might believe what is being said to them.

Guilt

After they have suffered the assault on identity, the subject will go through the stage. Throughout the identity crisis that has been created, the subject will be repeatedly told they are wrong. This is to create a strong sense of guilt. The subject will continue to be under attack for all the actions they have taken, no matter how large or small. The attack range can be broad. The subject may be criticised for their beliefs or the way they dress. Or even eating too slowly. They will begin to feel shame and guilt around their actions, and eventually, they will believe they are wrong. This can make them feel more vulnerable. They may also be more willing to conform to the new identity that the agent is trying to create.

Self-betrayal

Now that the subject believes that they're bad and that they should be ashamed of themselves, the agent will work with them to get them to admit it. The subject is feeling overwhelmed by guilt and disoriented at this point. The agent will attempt to force the subject into revealing his past identity. This can be done by continuing the mental attacks, threatening some serious physical harm, or both. This can be used to force the subject's friends, family, and peers to abandon their belief systems. It may take some time for this to happen, but the subject will feel betrayed by those whom he holds dear. This will only make the subject feel even more ashamed and lose his identity.

Breaking Point

This is when the subject feels disoriented and very depressed. The subject may be asking "Where are you?" You might ask, "Who am I?" What should you do? At this moment, the subject is having an identity crisis and is feeling deeply ashamed. The subject will have a nervous breakdown because they have been trumping all of his beliefs and those he has known since childhood. This can be described as a series of severe symptoms that indicate psychological problems. Some symptoms include disorientation, depression, and uncontrolled crying. You may also feel like you are completely lost. This is when the subject loses their sense of self. The agent can do anything they want with the subject at this point. In order to help the subject change their beliefs, the agent will offer them various temptations. The new system is designed to bring relief to the subject from the misery they are feeling.

Possibility of Salvation

After the agent has successfully broken down the self of their subject, it's time to move on. The next step is to offer salvation to the subject, but only if they choose not to hold on too tightly onto their old beliefs and embrace the one being presented. The subject is allowed to explore the world around him and is told that they would feel better if he or she followed the new path. The brainwashing stage includes four steps. These are leniency (compulsion to confess), channeling the guilt and releasing the guilt.

Leniency

Leniency means the "I'm able to help you" stage. The subject is now being disowned and they are forced to abandon the beliefs and people they hold on to for so long. They have been told that their actions are wrong and they are bad. The subject will feel isolated and helpless in this world. They will be ashamed of all the negative things they have done and want to know where to turn. If they reach this stage, an agent may offer to help or give them some sort of release. This can often take the form of a reprieve or some small kindness. Agents can give food and water to their subject, or ask them questions about their home or loved ones. These small acts will not seem significant in the current circumstances of the subject, which can lead to a feeling of relief and gratitude towards the agent. These feelings can seem extreme in comparison to what the agent has done. In some cases, the subject may feel the agent has saved their lives rather than simply offering a service. This distortion works in the favor of the agent since the subject is now going gain loyalty to the agent over past events.

Confessions are compelled

After the agent has won the trust of their subject they will attempt to get them to confess. This stage is sometimes called the "You are able to help yourself" stage. During this stage, the subject can see the difference between their identity assault pain and the relief that they get from the sudden leniency. If the brainwashing process works, the subject may feel a need to return some of the kindnesses shown to him by the agent. If this happens, the agent will be capable of presenting the possibility of confession as a means to alleviate the subject's feelings of guilt and pain. The agent will then guide the subject through a process to confess all the sins and wrongs they have committed in the past. This will depend on how the past mistakes and wrongs affect the new identity. This will be useful if the subject is a war prisoner. They can then confess to the offenses committed while fighting for freedom in the other country. Even though they are not necessarily wrongs or crimes, they violate the new ideology which holds that the regime is always right. These must be acknowledged.

Guilty Channeling

Once the subject goes through the channeling stage of guilt, it is clear that they have been suffering for months. The brainwashing process is over by the time that the subject has reached this point. They are now able feel the guilt and shame they feel, but they have lost their meaning. They cannot tell you what they have done wrong to make this happen, but they will admit that it is wrong. The agent will use the subject's information to help explain why they feel the way they do. The agent will be capable of attaching the feeling of guilt to whatever the subject wants. If the agent wishes to replace a particular set of beliefs, the agent will convince the subject to abandon the old beliefs and take over the new system. This is where the contract between old beliefs and new beliefs is formed. The old belief system was created to correspond with psychological agony, while the new belief systems were created to allow the subject to escape from that agony. They will have to choose, but it's easy to see that subjects would prefer the new system for feeling better.

Releasing Guilt

This is when the subject realizes that their old beliefs or values are causing him pain. They have had enough of the shame and guilt they have felt for several months. They soon realize that the guilt they feel is not caused by anything that they have done. Instead, it is their beliefs. You can offer some relief to the person who is feeling guilty. They will also feel relief from the realization that they are not a bad person. They now know that the problem isn't in them, but their belief systems and people around them. It is what they can do to get well again. They now know that they have an escape route by simply changing their belief system and accepting the one being offered. To let go of their guilt, all they have to do is denounce the people and institutions that were associated with their old belief system. The subject has control over this stage. They will be able realize that it is their responsibility to release all guilt. The only thing the subjects need to do to get out of this stage is to admit to any wrongdoings they may have done that were related to their old belief system. The subject will have successfully completed their psychological rejection of the former identity once they have admitted to all the details. The agent will then need to intervene in order to give the subject a new identity.

Chapter 9: Covert Emotional Manipulation

People are able to use deceitful and subversive techniques to manipulate emotions. These people seek to change your behavior and thoughts without even realizing they are doing it. This means that they can manipulate your perceptions in a way that makes you believe that it is your free will. Because you are not aware that it's happening, covert emotional manipulation is considered "covert." These people are skilled at manipulating emotions without your conscious awareness. They can use these techniques to hold you "psychologically captive".

Highly skilled manipulators will set their sights on your heart and get you to give them power over you emotional well-being, your self-worth, and your self-worth. They will manipulate you without you knowing it. They will gain your trust and you'll begin to value what they think of. After you let them in to your life they will start chipping away at the core of your identity. As you age, your self-esteem will drop and you will be able to become anything they want.

Hidden emotional manipulation is more common that you might think. Because it's subtle, people rarely notice that it's happening. In fact, in some cases they might not even be aware. This manipulation can be detected only by keen observers.

It is possible to know someone who used be joyful and fun. It could be that she was once in a relationship with someone else and now has a completely different personality. Even if the friend is old, it might be hard to recognize the change in her personality. This is the extent of covert emotion manipulation. It can change a person's whole outlook without them realizing. The manipulator will gradually chip away at you. You will accept tiny changes that slip under the radar, until an old version of yourself replaces you.

Covert emotional manipulation works as a slow-moving military coup. It requires you to make gradual concessions to your manipulator. It means that you are willing to make small concessions to the manipulative person in order for them to be able take control of your identity.

The manipulative person will push you to change small ways because you don't want "sweat" the small stuff. However, there is a domino effect when you start to give in to their demands. You will be more comfortable making further concessions. Your personality will also be destroyed and replaced in a gradual progression.

Social dynamics can be affected by emotional manipulation. Let's see how it plays in romantic relationships, friendships, or at work.

Emotional manipulation of relationships

It is possible to manipulate romantic relationships emotionally, even though it may not be malicious. Some women attempt to influence men's behavior to make them less "housebroken". That is perfectly normal. Some manipulations are malicious in that the manipulator has a desire to dominate or control another person.

Positive reinforcement is the most common technique used to manipulate romantic relationships. Your partner can manipulate you into doing what he wants. This is done by giving praises, flattering, giving attention, offering gifts, or acting affectionately.

Even the best things in relationships can end up being covert manipulation tools or props. To reinforce a certain behavior in your girlfriend, intense sex could be used. To reinforce certain behaviors, men can use charm and appreciation or gifts.

For control of their partners, skilled manipulators may use what psychologists call "intermittent positiv reinforcement." The victim will be given intense positive reinforcement by the perpetrator for a time and then the perpetrator will return to the victim's normal level of attention and appreciations. After a random period of time, he'll return to the intense positive reinforcement. It is taken away when the victim has become used to the special therapy. After she becomes comfortable with standard treatment, the special therapy is returned and everything seems random. The victim will now be "addicted to" the special therapy. Yet, she is unsure how to obtain it. In order to get it, she follows the instructions of her perpetrator and does whatever he wants. She hopes that one of the things she does will give her the intense positive reinforcement. This is how she becomes subservient.

You can also use negative reinforcement techniques to manipulate your partner. One partner may withhold sex to get the other person in a certain way. You can also use techniques like the silent treatment or withholding affection and love.

False intimacy can be created by some people who are malicious and pretend to be open with you. They could tell you about their lives and share their fears. While they give the impression of trusting you, it could also be a way for them to convince you that they are responsible for your actions.

Manipulators use insinuations well-planned to influence you to act in a certain manner at the right time to alter your long-term behavior. These insinuations may be expressed verbally or through actions. It is commonly known as "dropping hint" in colloquial English. People are always trying to figure what the other person wants from a relationship. So manipulative people can drop hints so you will do what they want.

Though it's possible to drop hints, this is not always malicious. Your girlfriend may want you to propose. She might also leave out bridal magazines. Though they are not always malicious, insinuations that are malicious can be very harmful and can affect your self-esteem. Partner can insinuate that you are gaining weight. Your partner might suggest you aren't making enough or your cooking skills have been poor. People use hints in order to say things without saying, and do any number of other harmful things that can affect your self-esteem.

Emotional manipulatives in friendships

Casual relationships and friendships are prone to emotional manipulation. While companies are more likely to develop than romantic relationships over time, this just means it can take more time to find out if your close friends are manipulative. The manipulation of friendships can lead to confusion, even though friends may be well-meaning. Because even close friends may have social rivalries, this explains "frenemies."

The manipulative friends tend not to be aggressive but passive-aggressive. These friends will manipulate you into giving them what they want. They may involve mutual friends, rather than coming directly to you.

Passive aggression is a manipulation technique that denies you the chance to directly address any issue your friend raises. This is how you lose by default.

A friend might ask you to do a favor. She may instead approach you and ask you. It is very difficult to refuse a request from a friend. Everyone in your circle sees you as selfish when you say no.

Passive aggression can also include the use of silence to get you to agree to a request. Imagine one of your friends talking to everyone except you. It's going be very awkward for both of you. People will start asking questions and deciding who is right.

Friends can also subtly manipulate you using subtle insults. Sometimes, they will give you subtle compliments with hidden meanings. It's possible to realize the hidden meaning behind the compliment and make a poor judgment about yourself.

You may be manipulated by friends who plan to take you on a "powertrip" that will control your social interactions. Friends may insist that your every social interaction should be at their apartment, or another location of their choice. Friends who want to dominate friendships are likely to do so by claiming the "home ground edge" over you. They'll push you outside of your comfort zone to expose your vulnerabilities, so you can become more emotionally dependent upon them.

Manipulative friendships will exploit your friendship in an exaggerated way and to a great extent. They will ask you to do many favors and not give a damn about your time. These friends are great friends because they will always ask you for favors, then use excuses to make it easier for themselves.

Emotional manipulating at work

There are many reasons your colleague might want to manipulate and control you. Perhaps you're on the same path in your career and he wants you to look bad. He may be lazy or he just wants to keep you from all his responsibilities. Another possibility is that he's a sadist who just wants to see him suffer.

Workplace stress is one of the ways people can dominate others. They then stress them out and then immediately relieve that stress. Let's say you make an error in a report. Your boss calls you to discuss it. He makes a big fuss about your mistake and threatens that you will be fired. But towards the end, his boss changes gears, and reassures us that our job is safe as long as we do what he wishes. Because it makes people fearful and gives them a sense obligibility, this type of manipulation works.

Your colleagues may try to manipulate you by giving you small favors and reminding you about them each time they need something. A colleague may cover you for an error you made at work. This could be for months or even many years. He will make you feel guilty and indebted.

Chapter 10: Body Language And Microexpressions

We've covered many of the important aspects of using dark psychology methods and manipulation strategies. This chapter will explore how to gather information and analyze potential targets using microexpressions, body language and body language.

The art of manipulation involves listening to the words and actions of others. Research has shown that what people say is only a small part of what's happening in the world of human communication. The subconscious mind picks up things we don't notice and may show up later in ways we didn't expect. However, if you pay attention, you can begin to understand how another person communicates information using their body language and microexpressions. These terms will be defined more clearly so you know what we are referring to. Then we will examine more deeply how these signals are manifested in different situations.

It's possible to be unaware of the nonverbal communication you are using when people interact with you. You might be surprised. So, ask your friends to describe how they perceive you when they interact. Although they might make observations about your senses or make comments about you, it is likely that you will hear more about how your face and body move, what you say, and any other peculiarities about you. These aspects are as closely linked to you as your words. These elements are part your personality and communicate a lot about who you are without having to speak out.

This principle holds true for almost all human beings. We've discussed the need to monitor and track specific behavior in order gather information about potential targets. If you get up close and personal with your target, you'll be able to observe their behavior. Microexpressions can be very short expressions that are not long enough to register to the observer. These expressions are often called microexpressions. Sometimes they are about hiding true feelings after an expression is lost. Other times they are completely unconscious reactions that occur due to things happening around them. They communicate emotion just as well as regular facial expressions. However, they can be hard to spot unless one is really paying attention. Everything going on in your body other than what comes out of your mouth is called body language. You use gestures to communicate information. These include the way you move your hands when you speak, your eyebrow furrowing, and the crossing of your legs. This is especially true when you're meeting someone for the first time. It is important to notice microexpressions when you are trying to make a first impression.

Let's review some of our earlier examples to see what's going right through microexpressions. Also, pay attention to your body language.

As the new guy at the party, Nichole is trying to make an impression. She is the leader and she is loved by everyone around her. Nichole noticed you and has made a significant impact on the room. You have been able to establish a private conversation. We can see you both on the balcony enjoying a couple of beers. Which are your next moves?

The face is one the most expressive parts of our bodies and can reveal a lot about us if we pay attention. Common expressions like crying or smiling convey emotion in the main sense. However, microexpressions can be made by small movements of facial muscle. It is important not to focus on these and end up making your target feel uncomfortable. However, you should still practice making eye contact with Nichole so that you can notice how she behaves and reacts to you talking to him. Exercising too much eye contact can result in staring, which can be creepy. Instead, practice other gestures and don't feel that you have to look around at your surroundings.

As long as there is a balance, it won't come across as disinterest.

What is happening between her smiles Are her eyes searching for something? We can detect subtle clues when trying to create an emotion or mood. If someone is paying attention, they may notice these microexpressions. You need to notice any signs that she is not interested in what you are doing and take action quickly. These signs can include looking down and briefly releasing a smile before resuming it, slouched or disinterested postures, eyes that dart away, looking for an exit, and pursed mouths, which is similar to someone who is anxious or tense. Be aware that she may be trying politely to conceal her feelings. Make sure to allow for some space between you two, and then change the subject to something more general. Perhaps you were asking her questions that she wouldn't mind answering but you got signals and hesitations before she spoke. You could say something to her to let her know that you don't want them to feel pressured and that she should be happy. It can be a great help to reverse uncomfortable or uneasy emotions by being straightforward and honest with your words. Do your best to make her feel better. You can always try again later. She may be having a difficult time engaging with you because of something else going on. If you are serious about re-engaging with her, do not do anything to endanger that possibility. Sometimes it is just a matter if the timing is right.

However, you might be able to spot positive signs she may be trying to conceal how much she loves the interaction. These are excellent signs to look for. They will give you the assurance that your tactics have been successful in getting her to a point where she is comfortable revealing personal information. These signals come in many forms, with a few brief moments of wide-eyed smiles that she quickly calms down. She may be excited by the interaction but is trying to disguise it. If she is too eager to please you, she might not be trying to make it uncomfortable. But, remember that anxiety can cause people to smile and giggle excessively. When this happens, look for signs that she is smiling or excited. Genuine smiles have a positive effect on the skin around the eyes. Faking a smile is easier than it sounds. It doesn't reach the eyes. This expression is common in novels. The writer is trying convey the message that the person is not authentic and is not trustworthy.

When it comes to body communication, there are many things that you can infer from her posture and where she places her feet. Let her be herself and let her feel the world around you. You might be surprised at how much you can gauge a person's mood and feelings about you by her posture while you talk to them.

When you sit down together to have a chat, the first thing you should examine is how she is holding herself. When you are standing in an open space, how is your body aligned with hers? Your ability to assess her interest in you and willingness to share personal space will be greater if your shoulders are directed towards you. If her body is more like that of yours, she might not be comfortable. In this case, you need to guide the conversation towards more comfortable ground and broaden the discussion until you gain some points back.

Your body posture will tell you if she is having fun and is concerned about your appearance. If she is straightening her body and keeping her head in front of you when she speaks to you, she will be interested in the conversation. If someone crosses their arms/legs, it's usually a subconscious signal that they are anxious or feeling uncomfortable. They are trying to defend themselves or cover their heads. This can occur when someone feels like they have been exposed in any way or when someone wants to conceal vulnerability and seem natural. These are signs to look for and match them with the words being said. You should be able guess what she is feeling.

It is important to pay attention to your feet orientation. If the two of you are standing together, and not with a piece of paper between you, then that's it. If her feet are directed towards you, this would be a sign that she is interested in you and is comfortable sharing information. If her feet and shoulders are not pointing towards you, she might not be feeling relaxed. The further her orientation is away from you the more she feels uncomfortable with her surroundings. This is a strong sign that she doesn't care about you. Perhaps she should give up and try again. Keep in mind that it's possible for her to be communicating negative signals in your response.

Your level of comfort can be determined by the pace at which someone breathes. Slow breathing signals comfort, while rapid breathing can indicate anxiety and discomfort. You should be aware of signs that your target is experiencing discomfort. Keep it in mind, and take a step back if things don't improve. Don't make the engagement awkward. This will likely convey to your target that she is not interested and is put off by something she said. You might also tell her that your discomfort is being picked up. You may find that she is interested in more information, which could help to reduce her discomfort. It's great if you can do that one-off.

Chapter 11: Dark Psychology And Manipulation The Power Of Seduction

At its core, lirting refers to a conversation between two people that aims to express romantic or sexual affection. There is no need to be serious. You can exchange witty banter and many compliments. It could involve sitting close together and many other types interactions between you. Flirting can often lead to seduction. If someone is in a relationship with someone else, they may be in a relationship.

Flirting with someone can lead to a more sexual affair. It could escalate to a request to rent an apartment or go on a date.

Let's move on to seduction. Seduction can be used as a way to persuade or make someone more eager to have sex. It's often part of the attraction that two people have. This sets the scene for sex. This could be either a woman wearing lingerie after a long day at the office or a man telling her girlfriend how stunning her dress looks. Seduction is a method of communicating desire to another person. A perfect seduction process should be honest and not misleading. It is possible to have a sexual encounter with someone you are seducing that is mutually satisfying and even begin a romantic relationship.

What is dark psychology and where does seduction fall within it? The purpose of seduction is to seduce, harm, or benefit the other person. These motives all share one thing: Every form of seduction involves some level of affection.

Dark Seduction: Why?

Dark psychology seduction can work well. It can make the person you're interested feel excited, and even intrigued. You could consider it to be a form or persuasion. Persuasion, when done ethically, can benefit the person being persuaded. Persuaders may cause harm to victims but only think of their potential rewards. This is also true when seduction takes place.

A person with good intentions might use dark psychology as a way to seduce. They do not want to harm others but they are able to have fun. This person is most likely to marry because they bring joy to their partner and are able to share it with them.

Dark psychology can make someone seek harm simply because they enjoy the thrill in letting someone down. These people will seduce vulnerable people, and they enjoy seeing their partner's anxiety and fear transform into fear. They do not respect their partner and are often promiscuous.

Someone who is entirely self-serving in dark seduction may have results that fall somewhere between the well-intentioned maniacal and the well-intentioned. An uninformed seducer who is self-serving can cause great harm, mainly because they are not aware of the consequences.

This person is more likely to be unhappy if they can't have healthy relationships with their lovers.

Dark psychology isn't a way to seduce or do something that is naturally evil. It is simply a strategy which has proven more successful than others. This method can be used for seduction and will increase your chances to meet someone you like. Because they know exactly what they want, dark seducers will be more successful than others at getting what they want. Dark seducers are more successful because they know what their goals are. They don't accept convenience or loneliness and aren't wishy-washy.

Why are Dark Seducers So Dangerous?

Dark seducers may be dangerous focs. They are skilled in manipulating victims to fall for them. The problem is the dark seducer might not really be in love. The dark seducer has a purpose for the relationship. They may be seeking companionship, sexual pleasure or something else. They might not seek love.

If the victim won't give their desires, the seducer may leave. If the victim feels manipulated and refuses to have sex with the seducer, he/she will leave and look for a new victim.

The seducer doesn't care about the partner. True seducers only view the other person as a tool. This helps them achieve the pleasure they seek. Once the tool has been used up, the seducer will look for another person to perform the same task.

Dark seducers are able to move quickly between relationships or remain with partners for long periods of time. It depends on the situation and the length of time they can keep the victim under their control. Some victims are able quickly to defend their rights. It's more difficult for victims of dark seduction to flee if they are held under their thumb for too long.

This does not necessarily mean that the dark con artist can love their victim. This simply means the dark seducer is comfortable with the current state of affairs, and will use their mind-control techniques and powers to keep the victim safe.

Dark Seduction Techniques

There are many methods of dark seduction. However, the key to this method lies in creating excitement and joy among those you want to seduce. You have to seduce the person. Your goal is to make them fall in love with you. These techniques let you have fun, be witty, and make your partner feel like you are interested in them.

The Friendly Opener

This technique doesn't ask you to question "what's that sign?" "Come here often?"

This technique works best if there is an open-ended question. You could also say, "Hey. Can you please help my friend? You can see what's happening. The seducer posed a question which led to a lively, friendly conversation. The seducer doesn't feel overpowered nor intruded. A friend instead asked a question.

Do it a little.

This tactic focuses on showing off, and not bragging about, your social media success.

Make sure you dress up in a stylish watch or jewelry. Different clothes are important because it shows you are independent and confident. However, you don't have be too eager for the company to like you. Instead, show support by going out with friends to bars or flirting with them. You will both be seen as a challenger and friend by the women.

Be kind.

If someone you want to seduce seems pompous or trying hard, you can pretend that they are about to leave. They will be impressed that your not playing the game. It shows them that they don't need your attention and aren't as eager to play along. If they ask you for your permission, you have almost won.

You need to pay attention again. It seems like the person who is interested you is trying to get attention to you a lot harder then you are.

Send Mixed Signals

It doesn't necessarily have to interest you. They should not call you. It is possible that the person who you are most interested may reciprocate. It might be worth not making contact. Why? It is possible to appear detached. This can make your target more curious about you, or even more fascinated. It's about building self-worth. Everyone wants to have what they don't have. Playing harder is a way to grab someone's interest.

Give the Ego long strokes

Don't flatter someone until they become blue. Instead, be open-minded and agree with them. Get to know your partner and learn about their emotions. You will find it easy to identify with their belief in them as the main characters in their stories. Because we all believe it about ourselves, this is true. Each person is their own main character in the story of their life. It is possible to validate and satisfy someone simply by being part of their story. It will make them feel validated, secure, and validated. They will also enjoy you being there and be able trust you.

Taboo!

Most people feel thrill-seeking in some way. It does not mean that everyone is looking for dangerous situations and hard drugs to feel alive. We all seek excitement and inspiration from the taboo.

Influence through Sexting

Seduction refers to making someone fall for you. It's often used to induce sexual attraction. Because you are persuading people into giving their whole selves for your cause, seduction can be one of the most powerful persuasion techniques.

There are many ways to seduce. These methods work no mater who you are or what kind of person you're trying. These methods don't require much preparation.

Select the right person

Even though you are able to charm anyone, smart decisions can help you seduce more people. People who are shy and reserved should be considered. These people are more vulnerable, and they need to be heard. It's easy to seduce them, by giving them attention and taking them to the next stage.

Send mixed signals

This technique of seduction dates back to ancient times. Mixed signals can make people feel uncomfortable. People feel more attracted to the challenge presented when they are challenged. In this instance, it is you.

Create a need

You need to make the person you wish to seduce feel dependent on you. This need may be sexual or deeper. It is possible to create a need by making someone feel unhappy or anxious. This will make it easier for people to follow you.

False senses security

You create a bond when you feel safe around your partner. It is easier for you to convince them to do what it is that you want. Although this may seem like security, they will understand what you mean and be more likely to do what you ask.

Make Yourself Desirable

People don't like losing. People don't enjoy being around people who aren't interested in them. Make sure that you are surrounded by people you enjoy when you find someone you love. This creates an unease which makes them want you to move on as they fear losing your love.

Treat Yourself to a Treat

It is not a good idea for someone to tempt you into buying something that you regret later. This is true of everything, from food and careers to romantic relationships. This is what drives people nuts. This mindset is what allows you to obtain anything you want.

Utilize Suspense

You should pay them some attention but not all. This will make them competitive, just as when they are tempted. They will think only of you. You will influence every aspect of their life. This is what it is because you are in complete command.

Be mysterious

People love mystery. They are attracted to mystery and love to know the answers. You can seduce curious people by creating mystery. It is important not to divulge too much information. The mystery can be about any topic. Talking about your ex could make you a jerk or have a negative influence on the person that you're trying for. You can add mystery by looking into their eyes, smiling frequently, listening to their questions, and using a neutral voice.

You can subtly stand out by being yourself

It shouldn't be obvious that your goal should be to grab their interest. You want it to be clear that you are different because of who and how you are. Red lipstick, although it isn't unusual, makes women stand out. This is also true for men who wear bright or patterned ties. It is crucial to identify one element that sets you apart from the rest. That element should be natural.

Utilize Scents

Did you realize that people's scents can attract other people? It is important to know that people have their preferred scents. You should get to know the person before you use this technique. Scents can influence the subconscious.

It can reveal information about another person to someone without them being aware, which makes it one effective way to increase your seduction progress.

Take care to your assets

Physical attraction is crucial when it comes to seduction. Do not display your entire assets. This could cause a negative reaction. Stronger men may choose a shirt that has shorter sleeves. This allows the man they wish to seduce to see all of their assets, without making it obvious that they are trying too hard to impress.

To cover their chests, women might choose a fitted, below-the knee dress. You will be covered, but your target will still see your entire body.

These People Can Confuse You

When you first see them, you should pay attention to them. However, if they do not look at you, then only give them your full attention. This confuses them. It makes you even more mysterious. You don't want to drive the other person crazy.

Boldness, a virtue

If you're ready and willing to face the world, then it's time to be bold. Now you are convinced and they are yours. There is no reason not to act immediately. Grab the moment and let it go.

How to Avoid Dark Seduction

Dark seduction should be something you are aware of. Dark seduction can be used by men to gain confidence, avoid rejection, or to make it easier for them to meet women. These techniques are not popular with many people because they do not care about the other person. They have goals and will accomplish them, regardless who is hurt.

This can lead to serious consequences. Dark manipulators can use dark seduction methods to achieve their goals.

They will search for vulnerable victims, and then present the best solution. They might be able to assist a victim who is involved in a serious relationship.

The seducer can be charming, funny, and an ideal victim. While the victim may believe that they have found their soulmate or a true friend, the seducer only wants to make them happy. While it might last for a while the relationship will end soon, the seducer is not likely to return.

The victim will feel hurt, if not broken. The victim might have trusted the seducer to too much. Now, they are broken and hurt. They may be depressed or anxious and not trust others.

Dark seduction comes with many negative consequences. It is important that you are aware of these signs. You need to be aware of these signs if your experience dark seduction by a narcissist/psychopath. These people don't care much about the needs and well-beings of others. These people don't care much about the well being of others and are only concerned with their own needs.

Your perception of your partner's personality can greatly depend on the way they started their relationship. This includes the level of attraction and romance you shared as well the feeling that your relationship is in a good place. It will probably be too late to get out if things go wrong. This is especially true when the other person in the relationship does not know what they want. If you don't have a clear view, it can be difficult to decide whether you want to end the relationship.

Before you enter into a relationship, you must understand your goals. You'll be better prepared in case your relationship goes south. This will allow to you to see things as they really are, before you lose your self-worth.

This can prove to be difficult. If we aren't in a loving, committed relationship, it can make us feel worthless. When we don't feel connected, it is easy to jump into another relationship. Here are the problems.

Before entering into a new partnership, it is important to do some soul-searching.

There's no harm in being in a non-traditional relationship. It is possible to take some time for you, look at your life, and decide what kind of relationship you want.

This will allow you to determine the type and kind of relationship you are looking for. You shouldn't rush into a new partnership just because you feel lonely.

You'll set goals and be able to escape from the darkness seducer.

It is important to start by deepening the depth of your thinking and soul-searching. Then, you can decide on the details of what kind of relationship you want at this stage in your lives. Describe the expectations you have for your partner. Describe how this relationship should be. Make sure to set clear boundaries.

Chapter 12: Who Can Be Impacted By Dark Psychology

We must next consider the possibility of being affected by dark psychology. People with certain traits are generally more vulnerable than those without them. They are also known as empaths.

What is an Empath, and what does it do?

Empaths, who are sensitive individuals, can sense the energy and emotions in others. They are able to take on the feelings and make them theirs.

If you're an empath, you may find it difficult to have clear boundaries. This is because you absorb the stress of others. But if your energy is positive and you are careful about the people around you, you will attract people who are happy and joyful. These positive emotions are easily absorbed into your everyday life.

Scientists have long believed that people can feel what other people are feeling. It is called 'emotional contagion' when people copy the emotions of others. Hatfield, 2009 says that it is quite common.

You can think about how much it drains you to be around people who constantly complain. You might start the conversation in the most positive mood but soon find yourself in a downward spiral. Sometimes they end the conversation feeling much better than you, but sometimes you feel awful. You might be in a bad mood. It is likely that a cheerful friend will make you smile. Even if empaths are not your thing, it's likely that you have felt this way at one time or another.

Mirror neurons will be in place, which will allow us to feel what the other person is feeling when we look at how they are acting. If we watch someone complete an action, the brains of those regions will activate. It is possible for our brains to react the same way as we would if we were actually doing the action. This means that we can feel what other people are feeling quite well (Marsh 2012.

Some people may experience mirror-touch syndrome, which is even more alarming. It's a condition where their tactile and visual senses get confused. They can feel that someone is touching them by simply being able to see another being touched (Medina und DePasquale 2017.

Most of us will be capable of empathizing with others at some level, but Dr. Elaine Aron, author of The Highly Sensitive Person, says that people who are sensitive to extremes of emotion will account for 15 to 20%. These people will have a more sensitive nervous system and will be more able to empathize.

While some children are born naturally sensitive to touch, many of these empaths also have the benefit of having had a childhood that was more nurturing. Children who have been through trauma can learn new strategies to help them survive, adapt, and thrive in ways other children might not be able.

These mechanisms of survival, although some may not work well when they reach adulthood, can still serve their purpose when they're used from a more empowered perspective. As an adult, empaths will find themselves in an unusual position: they must navigate through a world which may invalidate or reject some experiences and still expect them to gain empathy wisdom.

Most empaths will have many positive attributes. You'll learn how to utilize the many options and techniques that are available to an empath in order to make a positive difference in the world. Be aware that empathic qualities can be accompanied by a powerful and dark undercurrent.

An empath can tap into emotions. This can help them get more out life.

An empath is a person who can see the world from many perspectives. This type of personality is often misunderstood. Although some people may try to hide this ability, others will learn more and be able to leverage it in a variety of ways.

Empaths are Emotional Detectives

The empath can enter any room to read the contents right away. They can be sensitive to subtle facial expressions and changes as well as shifts in voice and body language.

It is a sign that they are able to quickly establish rapport with others and communicate in a way that is easy for everyone.

The problem is that not all empaths are created equal. Many of us were told as children that we were sensitive to certain things. You might have tried to mask what was unique about yourself as an empath to learn how socially acceptable.

Instead, you can notice if any of these natural characteristics are present when you're in a new social setting. Does your personality make you feel comfortable around people of all backgrounds? Do you find it easy and enjoyable to converse with people? This indicates that you are sensitive and flexible with other emotions.

If you find these tasks difficult, continue to read about this topic. Dale Carnegie's book "How to Win Friends & Influence People" is one of the most well-known.

How to Identify Toxic Empaths

Because empaths can provide support, energy, and resources for their victims, malignant narcissists tend to focus on empaths. Empaths can raise the energy of those around them through a lot more emotional labor and ability. Narcissists will be able to recognize some of the unique gifts and abilities that empaths have and will work to get as many resources as possible for their own purposes and needs.

You can think about it like this: Toxic people can use empaths as a way to bypass their failures and help them heal. They will be free to use some of their empathic compassion to let go of any bad behavior they choose without feeling responsible. They will capitalize on the empath's capacity to adapt, and the resilience they possess to trap them in a destructive cycle.

These are all done in order to make sure the narcissist is able to get what they want. They won't be concerned about how much it will hurt or drain them.

Empowered empaths learn to accept responsibility for their behavior and can identify manipulative behavior.

Asking questions is a great way to spot someone who is harmful.

*A

*B

*C

Empaths Could Be Emotional Sponges

Many dark psychologists prefer empaths to work with because they can take all their negativity, regrets, or other details about their actions, and pass it on to the other person. And empaths will often accept all of it, including the guilt and shame, without knowing why. The person who did the deed will feel better as they were able release the empath from their burden, and the empath will suffer.

An empath needs to be able to establish healthy boundaries for himself. You don't want this to happen and then someone else takes advantage of your ability to empathize with you.

Questions are a good way to spot someone using you as an emotional sponge.

*A

*B

*C

Most Empaths Don't Know Their Power

Many people don't realize that they have this trait. Sometimes, they are too focused on helping other people rather than healing their own past abuses or trauma.

An empath will thrive if they surround himself with fellow empaths. Empaths will soon discover that it is possible to be both spiritually and scientifically at the same time.

Empathic ability is a key to unlocking your potential to harness the power of your intuition to help you get more. It is important to recognize your strengths and find others with them in order to get the best results. It will make a big difference in your personal and professional life.

Chapter 13: Emotional Intelligence

Emotional intelligence means the ability understand, use, control and manipulate one's emotions. It can be used to ease anxiety, help others, make decisions, solve problems, and resolve conflict. Emotional intelligence can help you build better relationships, achieve your career and personal goals, as well as academic and professional success. It can be used to help you communicate with your emotions, set your intentions, and make informed decisions about what's most important to your life.

The following four characteristics are commonly used to describe emotional intelligence.

1. Self-control – You can control your impulsive thoughts or actions, handle emotions in healthy and positive ways, take action, keep your promises, and adjust to changing conditions.

2. Self-awareness – You are aware and conscious of your emotions and how they impact your thoughts, actions and decisions.

3. Empathy - Your social consciousness includes empathy. You can read and understand the thoughts and feelings of other people, as well as their worries and hopes.

4. Relationship management - You will learn how to establish and maintain positive relationships, connect effectively with others, empower and influence them, work effectively together, and resolve conflict.

What is emotional intelligence and its significance?

We all know the truth that even the brightest people are not always the most fulfilled and popular. Most of us know someone who is not only academically gifted but also socially inept, and who fails to make friends or work well. Intelligence, also known as the intelligencequotient (IQ), doesn't guarantee success in your life. Although your IQ may help you get to college, your emotional intelligence will help deal with the emotions and tension of final exams. Both EQ & IQ can be used in conjunction and they work best together.

Emotional intelligence affects:

Your work and school performance. You will be able to manage the social challenges in the workplace, motivate and lead others and have a high level of emotional intelligence. Many companies now regard emotional intelligence as as important as technical ability when evaluating potential job candidates and use EQ testing prior to hiring.

Your physical well-being. If you can't control your feelings, likely, you can't control your tension. This could cause serious health issues. Uncontrolled stress can lead to serious health problems. It can raise blood pressure, suppress your immune system, increase the risk of strokes and heart attacks, and cause infertility. Being able to manage stress is the first step towards increasing your emotional intelligence.

Your mental well-being. Stress and uncontrollable emotions can cause anxiety and depression. If you are unable to accept, control, or understand your emotions, you will find it difficult develop strong relationships. This can make you feel depressed or lonely and worsen any mental health problems.

Your friendships. It will make you more comfortable communicating your feelings and understand the emotions of others. This helps you connect better and develop deeper relationships in your professional as well as personal lives.

Your social awareness. It is important to be able to feel your emotions and interact with the people around you. Social intelligence can help you tell a friend or a foe, to gauge their interest in you, to minimize tension, to control your nervous systems through social contact, as well as feel loved and comfortable.

There are four key skills that will help you increase your emotional intelligence.

Emotional intelligence is a combination of skills that can easily be learned. It is important to recognize that there is a difference between learning about EQ or applying it to your everyday life. It doesn't matter if your mind is clear that you need to do anything, but it doesn't mean that you will. It is important to maintain emotional awareness by learning how to reduce tension in the moment. You can also learn how to modify your actions to stand up to pressure.

These are the essential skills that can increase your EQ as well as improve your ability control emotions and communicate effectively with others.

1.Self-management

2.Self-awareness

3.Social awareness

4.Relationship management

Building emotional intelligence,

1: Self-management

To be able make well-informed decisions about your actions and engage your EQ, it is important to be able rely on your feelings. You will lose control over your emotions and be less able to think critically and do things properly if you're anxious.

Imagine a moment when you were overwhelmed by tension. Is it difficult to think clearly and make a well-informed decision? It's unlikely. You can't think objectively or correctly assess feelings when you are stressed.

Emotions are essential pieces of information that you can use to tell yourself about others. However, if we are confronted by tension that forces us outside our comfort zone, we can lose control and become frustrated. You can learn to accept disturbing information and not let it control your emotions or self-control. If you are able handle tension and remain emotionally present. You'll be able manage your impulsive feelings and actions by making decisions, following through on commitments and adapting to changing situations.

2: Self-awareness

Stress management is just one step in gaining emotional intelligence. Attachment psychology suggests that your present emotional experience is a direct result of your childhood experience. Your ability to deal with core emotions like fear, sadness and joy will also depend on the quality and consistency of your early emotional experiences. Your emotions can be valuable assets when you are older if your primary caregiver was able to recognize and cherish your feelings as a child. On the other hand, if you found your emotional interactions as children confusing, threatening or traumatic, it's likely that you have tried to separate yourself emotionally from these feelings.

Understanding how emotion affects thoughts and behavior is not easy. You need to be able to have a moment-to–moment interaction, or connect with your emotions.

Are there feelings that flow? Do you experience one emotion after the next as your circumstances change.

Are you experiencing physical sensations such as a tightness in your chest, stomach, or throat due to emotions?

Do you experience distinct emotions like rage, sorrow and fear?

Can you feel powerful emotions that attract attention to yourself and others?

Do they play a role in the decision making process? Are you in control of your emotions

These emotions may not be present if you've never had them before. It's important to connect with your core emotions, accept them, and relax to improve emotional stability. Meditation and mindfulness are two ways to achieve this.

Mindfulness is the practice of intentionally focusing on the present moment while not passing judgment. Mindfulness cultivation originated in Buddhism. But, meditation and prayer are common practices across all religions. Mindfulness helps you shift from thinking to focusing on the present moment. You will gain a greater perspective on your life and be able to appreciate your emotions, physical and mental experiences. Mindfulness will help you relax, concentrate, and increase your self-awareness.

Emotional knowledge development

Learning how to deal with stress is crucial in order to feel at ease. You can also reconnect with intense or negative emotions and change how you react to them. HelpGuide has a free Emotional Intelligence Toolskit to help improve your emotional sensitivity.

3: Social awareness

Use social awareness to interpret and understand nonverbal cues that others use when they interact with you. These signals tell you how people feel, what they value, and how their emotional state changes over time.

It is possible to read and understand power dynamics and emotional experiences of others by listening to their nonverbal cues. You are socially tolerant and empathic.

Mindfulness is a tool to increase emotional and social awareness.

To increase social awareness, mindfulness is essential in order to be mindful. To be able to recognize subtle nonverbal signals, you must first understand the importance of mindfulness in the social process. Being socially conscious requires that you be present in the moment. Multitasking, which many of us love, can cause you to miss subtle emotional shifts from others that can help your understanding.

* You can be more likely achieve your social goals by putting aside all thoughts and focusing on the interaction.

* Monitoring the emotional response of another person is a two-way process that can help you be more aware of emotional changes.

* Being more aware of others does NOT mean you are less conscious of yourself. Listening to other people can help you gain insight about your emotional state, values, beliefs and more. Listening to other viewpoints can help you learn about yourself.

Conclusion

These observations lead us to conclude that social norms as well as laws and morals for human beings are not normal. Society often encourages group behavior, which is driven by the need to dominate the weak over the powerful. The culture of survivalism has become the standard. What society wants to do is to control the wild beast that is every human being by informing them at a young age how to comply with the laws, rules, morality, and regulations of the ruling community. These are generally the wealthy people who run our governments and institutions. If society does not treat them fairly, should we condemn them? When, in reality, their ability to thrive in hostile environments where wealth, education, or family is a determining factor of one's privilege? Isn't psychology time to step out of its shell and recognize that normal human behavior contradicts rigid society rules and regulations? People hate society. However, they feel helpless trying to survive among the sheep. They are powerless against those who regulate morality and law-making. It shouldn't surprise that every now and again, one person will decide to alter the society or their environment to have a more controlled existence and not be bound by the rules of societies which, as we all know, are subject to a constant collapse and re-invent themselves. China transformed from a poor empire to a military-controlled regime, then to a communist government in the 1950s that emphasized fair living conditions for all. Then to the China we see today. This socialist capitalist state is based on a ruling Party that decides the lives of those without power. China is likely to see another revolution. It is difficult to believe at the moment given the turmoil in many places caused by minorities that are required to follow the central rules. Both empires are blinded by their doom! How can psychology address the idea of human activity being a survival mechanism? That humans are inherently hostile, cruel, and oppressive to weaker people? The role of psychiatrists in mental institutions is often one of social control. If you refuse to comply with society's laws, you will be deemed psychotic and should be committed for the safety and benefit of all.

Psychology is, however, seen as the liberating aspect of mental health. We help people who have lost touch with society to integrate into what is common for their age. How will society respond to those who want to rebel against their environment and live a life they love? Or are we content to wait for the catastrophes shown in movies to unfold, ushering in survivalism - true social norm - to return to a dog-eats-dog lifestyle?